The Great Grandmother Light

New and Selected Poems

Also by Joe Weil

Painting the Christmas Trees, Texas Review Press, 2008

What Remains, Nightshade Press, 2008

The Plumber's Apprentice, NYQ Books, 2009

The Great Grandmother Light

New and Selected Poems

Joe Weil

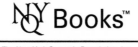

The New York Quarterly Foundation, Inc.
New York, New York

NYQ Books™ is an imprint of The New York Quarterly Foundation, Inc.

The New York Quarterly Foundation, Inc.
P. O. Box 2015
Old Chelsea Station
New York, NY 10113

www.nyqbooks.org

First Edition

Set in New Baskerville

Layout and Design by Raymond P. Hammond

Cover Illustration © 2013 by Simone Kearney | www.simonekearney.com

Library of Congress Control Number: 2013949223

ISBN: 978-1-935520-80-1

The Great Grandmother Light

New and Selected Poems

Acknowledgments

The author wishes to thank Phoebe Davidson of Palanquin Press, Dwyer Jones, and Hersch Silverman of Beehive Press who collected poems into broadsides and pamphlets for various readings through the 1980s and 1990s. The author is especially grateful to Dave Roskos, who published many of the poems that later appeared in subsequent books in the chapbooks *A Portable Winter* and *The Pursuit of Happiness* (Iniquity Press/Vendetta Books). Thanks to Paul Ruffin for permission to reprint poems from *Painting the Christmas Trees* (Texas Review Press). Grateful acknowledgement to the following publications in which most of these poems first appeared in one form or another: *Arbella, Arc of a Cry* (now Circus Books), *Big Hammer, Big Scream, Best American Poetry blog, Blue Collar Review, Boston Review, Caduceus, Cartographer Electric, Edison Literary Review, Ink Well, Journal of New Jersey Poets, Lips, Long Shot, Louisiana Review of Literature, MAGGY, New York Quarterly, North American Review, Paddlefish, Patterson Literary Review, Red Brick Review, The Red Room, The Saranac Review, The New York Times, The Star Ledger,* and *Tiferet.* Some of these poems have been reprinted in the following anthologies: *Bum Rush the Page, Identity Lessons, The Poets of New Jersey, What's My Exit,* and *Working Words.* Finally, Weil wishes to thank Maria Mazziotti Gillan, who helped in so many matters that have been instrumental to his survival as an artist.

For my wife, the poet Emily Vogel,
and our daughter Clare

Contents

from Painting the Christmas Trees

from The Plumber's Apprentice

New and Uncollected Poems (2006–2013)

Prelude

"I want this hardened arm to cease dragging its cherished image."
—Rimbaud

This is my arm
dragging its cherished image:
A copse of flowers
the blue of a jet flame;
and this is my hand,
writhing into the void,
pulling up rabbits,
the beloved dead,
the tools of my tirade.

Anvils! Cries the self.
More Light!
A stone!

But what is it making?

The soul chirps feebly,
a lone cricket in November.
On the roadside
lost in yellowing grass,
in dead leaves
already turned to mulch
this stray persistent flesh
weaves on,
ends and begins
where desire
bends the trees
and turns
the body back again.

Ben Hur

This is the part where
Charlton Heston's sister gets cured of leprosy

Charlton cries
I swallow a fig Newton

Last time I saw *Ben Hur*
I was twelve years old
My parents were still alive
Moths swarmed around the porch light,
Refrigerator hummed,
We were safe
        Now I'm thirty
Rocky and Clare
        in a grave
I start to cry
        because Charlton
is hugging his sister and he's home
and I'm not
and it's raining
inside the movie
      and out
Outside, the smell of wet dirt
and soggy garbage
        wafts through my window
Shit!
      If I had a girlfriend
we'd screw till the moon was cheese
we'd create our own epic:
thighs, breasts, mole hairs, freckles,
all the noises peculiar to coupling
hips rounding into air, hands palming
flesh, flesh so smooth and rough and sweaty
and...

The theme music flares
I know it's a corny flick
I've read Rimbaud
but I'm sad and full of
fig Newtons
it's late and
    my hairline's receding

outside the rain keeps falling
looks like a thousand needles
Falling under
    the streetlights glare,
piercing space
and I wish
    I were dead or in the arms of a girl
I hear the soft incessant hum of a refrigerator,
the soft incessant hum of me
falling through space, falling asleep
with my hand between my legs.

The Mangling of the Rose

Dawn stretched forth her fingertips of rose.
It was at that early hour when as a child
I watched *Davey and Goliath.*
"A Mighty Fortress Is Our God," I sang.
Elizabeth's streets were deserted.
Not even one wino stirred.
I stood reflected in a florist window.
That's when I saw a disgusting sight,
a display of floral sexuality
I did not know could exist.

For I saw a rose, a single crimson rose,
fingering itself in livid hot abandon
(In full view of the gladiolas no less!)
It turned redder, almost purple in its lust.
I said: Ho rose! Fie thee!
This is not consummate with thy tradition.
Quit playing with thyself!
Thou art the rose, symbol of the virgin.
For thee, the martyrs shed sweet blood.
Knights trampled fields and streams,
slew dragons,
suffered trials for thy sake—

Ooh, ooh, the rose replied, I'm sick of being
some lame excuse for poets of western civ.
Do you know how lonely it gets day after day
not even one bee to buzz my petals?
Go away! Leave me alone,
I'm not hurting anyone.
I bet that you're repressed!

I walked away.
What else was there to do?
Later that day,
I attended a charity lawn benefit

in Short Hills, New Jersey:
There was a string quartet playing Haydn,
gynecologists in white tuxedos,
wives in summer Halston gowns.
Oh, it was a lovely gathering!
I forget whether it was for MS
or for saving the baby seals
but we were all schmoozing about
drinking good champagne
when the roses attacked.

It was five in the afternoon.
It was exactly five in the afternoon.
They came over the Garden wall
in full battle fatigues,
doffing their bright berets,
clicking their thorns
in terrifying synchronization.
Ah the terrible din of those thorns,
I'll remember the rest of my days!
For I saw an orthodontist
impaled on the Quartet's cello.
I watched a second cousin twice removed
of Gloria Vanderbilt
get thrown to the well-trimmed lawn
and smothered by a multi-vicious Roosevelt.
We claim Short Hills, the leader said,
We claim Short Hills for the revolution!

The yard smelled like a thousand funerals
all gathered in one place.
The only thing that saved us
was the ambiguity
of the rose's demands.
They couldn't figure out
whether they were for the Jews

19

or against them,
whether Trotsky or Mao
was their spiritual impetus.
Is this infrastructure?
one of the roses asked.
My God, I have to know!

In lieu of a paradigm
they drank all the champagne,
spared the truffles,
honored the strawberries as kin.
Finally, they arrived at three demands:
One, they wanted an escort to the airport.
Two, they wanted soil, lots of soil.
Three, they wanted Sissy Spacek's phone number.

The state police arrived along with the marines.
They showed no mercy.
Roses fell everywhere,
leaves crumbled to the lawn.
One dying rose began to sing a revolution song.
A rose is a rose is a rose, it sang,
and not Goddamn metaphor!

I came out from under the pâté
traumatized and stunned,
for who would have thought
the roses harbored such hostility,
that they had waited all these years
to avenge themselves?
On the stem of one dead tea rose
lay all the T-shirt slogans of the world:
Free Mandela! Kill Mandela!
Save the sperm whale!
Vote Nixon! Trotsky is our God!
Give arms to the Contras!

Happy, happy thoughts!
Hitler's cool!
Anti nuke!
Better dead than red!
Down with the Middle Class!
Duran Duran!
Jesus saves!
Grateful Dead!
Pepsi! Pepsi!
Disney World!
You poor confused little flower, I said.

I walked away then.
What else was there to do?
Sick with the stench of roses,
head full of isms, strong convictions,
and devoid of poetry.
I thought of the rose of Dante.
The Romance of the Rose.
The Legend of the Roses infinite unfolding,
its petals curled around eternity.
I conjured up the signets of the age,
the calligraphic rose that framed,
caressed the script of Gothic bibles.
I saw the Rose of Sharon,
my own dim heritage
then thought how this is the century
in which roses mean nothing.

This Is How the Moon Will Know Us *(A Lullaby)*

This is how the moon will know us
when we are dead or almost dead or near
some strange equivalent thereof:
It will know us most unknowingly
as a leaf in the dark caresses of a child's face.
It will string up the sea like a lyre and play
the dark glissando of waves.

Oh hips
rose startled
and sublime!
It will feel
most impossibly
deep
the needles and pins
that prick our unhappy lives.

I swear
the moon has no need
for beatitude or praise.
I have seen it
in an irrigation ditch
making a holy thing
of filthy water.

This is how the moon will know us
when we are dead or almost dead or near:
It will feel the deep divinity we bear,
night's air.

Love Poem in Stump Time

Your toes are a pale yellow
and have that hard, U-shaped ridge of skin
common to feet
that sweat a lot.
We are in a diner in New Jersey
late.
The waitress looks as if her feet
might resemble yours.

I know now my whole life is owed
to women with feet like this:
calluses, bunions, ingrown nails.

As if a wound could be a doorway to
some sense of kindness
beyond the crap
something undeniably
                          real
as if only the tired were
capable of love.

You're tired. So I stroke your feet
under the table
propped in my lap
ten digits worth of crow.

The waitress serves our bagels
one eyebrow arches as she takes
pencil stub to pad.
And I love you
                love you
through the doorway
        of every wound.

The Glueman

I scraped the glue off my
Father's work shoes
Every day for thirty years
And when he was dead
And sufficiently prayed over
By the Knights of Columbus
And the Holy Rosary Society
I went to work:

I built his effigy out of glue,
And he stood in the yard
A wonder to all the neighbors,
The glueman,
A monument to glue.

His ex-boss came by
And was impressed.
He offered me a thou.
"Good PR," he said,
"We'll stick him in the parking lot."
I told him to give me a week to think about it
And then he drove away agreeing to that.

I had more glue
So I went to work:

I sculpted a time clock
And constructed the mortgage,
And failure to pay the mortgage,
The extra job,
Driving a taxi,
The severed thumb
He'd lost to a compactor,
My mother's old dresses
From the Salvation Army,
The asses he kissed,
Including that boss's.

And I made Uncle Sam
With the wings of an eagle
And the tail of a serpent.
Uncle Sam was well-hung and desired
To dick some poor boy
Up the ass.
So I made the draft notice,
And the frozen landscape of Korea,
And the shitty UN-issued rifles
That didn't work, and my dad, eighteen,
Frightened, freezing,
And the corpses of Chinamen
Piled high on the border.
And I made the lungs of my father
Ruined by breathing
That glue for thirty years.

And a week passed.
And the boss came back.

"What's all this shit?" he asked.
"I offered to buy the statue, not all this shit."
I told him there was no charge for the extra.
"I don't want it," he said,
"Just give me the statue."
And I told him I couldn't break up the set.
If he wanted the statue, the rest came with it.
So he called me a fool
And he drove away.

The Blue Woman

In memory of Willie Weatherspoon, who froze to death.

At first I hated all the assholes
Driving by in their cars,
Screaming, "Get a job, motherfucker."
Then I got used to it.

I got used to the garbage,
The half-finished drumsticks
Of Kentucky Fried.

On warm autumn days,
I'd sit on the steps of the library,
Taking in the sun.

That blueness you get to a sky when it's fall
Was the most beautiful thing I'd ever seen,
And I used to dream there was a woman,
This Blue Woman—someone to sink into
At the end of the day.

I dreamed the Blue Woman's cunt
Was as dogwood blossoms,
That pink grown into red,
And her lips were like the
Powdered wings of moths.

And I lay on the steps of that library,
And closed my eyes,
And felt the heat of her body
Gliding over mine.

When I dreamed,
I thought no winter,
But winter came,

And I hid myself
Under newspapers,
And I knew I wasn't human anymore.

Who'd kiss an unreal man?

Look at these hands.
You can see the streets through them.
Look at these feet.
I'm not human anymore.

There ought to be a law.
When you stop being real,
But no suffering allowed.
But I still hurt, I still scream,
and now I can't find me
my Blue Woman,
and she's the only thing
made sense.

There's got to be something
makes sense—
her lips
like the powdered wings of moths.

Now I can't find her.
God strike me dead.
Be merciful and kill me.

Cover me with newspapers,
put the Earth over my head,
but let me feel the breath
of that Blue Woman
once more before I die.

Refusing the Sea

White-crested, the green waves wallop you
though you stand gull stoic and watch them foam,
and hardly blink, as if a pair of wax wings
grew from your back, and you rose to fit the air,
vagrant, and at ease, your long hair riffling every wind,
blue fired bright, drawn out from the kiln of the sun.

And what is this oppressive heaviness
towards which you pit the gravity of your stare?
How long will it hold you? This shore
line turns and shifts, the pebbles grabbed from under you
by the magician sea, a tablecloth
from which the glass days are upended,
until you're the only thing left standing,
alone, so fiercely alone, utterly
content to spoil the tricks of the sea
which wants only to make you weightless in its arms,
wants only what you want, and you refuse.

from **What Remains**

Teaching the Dead

Come, Ma, and I will teach you
how to pray,
now that you're dead,
now that you sweep the grave's floor
with the fringes of your nightgown
and beg the moon for one last
drink.

I will teach you the alphabet
of my body.
This is what we are always doing—
this love
grown outward like a prayer,
this language
that's a necklace of bear's teeth,
a bracelet of whalebone,
this life gone north from the eyes.

We, who are always coming and going,
who are only a little while
here
must dance.

I will teach you
the round stones of memory,
the moist palms in which they hide.
Guess which hand I hold my grief in
and the space will open up between us.

This is a wound that freely opens.
Two coins for your eyes, Ma, two coins
and an old black shoe heel

to toss into the dark street—
the lights just coming on.

Morning at the Elizabeth Arch

The winos rise as beautiful as deer.
Look how they stagger from their sleep
as if the morning were a river
against which they contend.

This is not sentiment
filled with the disdain
of human pity.
They turn in the mind,
they turn
beyond the human order.

One scratches his head and yawns.
Another rakes a hand
through slick mats of thinning hair.
They blink and the street litter moves
its slow, liturgical way.
A third falls back
bracing himself on an arm.

At river's edge, the deer stand poised.
One breaks the spell of his reflection
with a hoof and, struggling,
begins to cross.

Hopper's Shoes

That's them, over there,
in the corner,
casually monumental,
like everything else
he ever painted.

The afternoon sun
leeches
colors from the room,
from the walls, laundry,
a coat draped over
a spoke-back chair.

The naked lady seated
primly on the edge
of the well-made bed
is tired.

Her back's sore.
She would like an apple.
She would like a copy of
True Detective magazine.

Hopper never set out
to capture "Human Loneliness."

It bored him.

He wanted his figures
to look on
with the rows of
potted geraniums,
look on with the windows
of all the frame houses.

"Light," he wrote,
"is the absence of blood."

First Memory

I remember the delicious heaviness
of an old yellow cab,
the thick, green leather upholstery
cracked and torn
as if a giant moth
had hatched from it.

Now, taking this road
inwards toward morning,
waking to sorrows
like poems
worn out from reading,

I step down these cellar stairs

to a place where it's always cool,
smelling of turpentine
and mold,
the pipes like soldiers
at Valley Forge—
wrapped in rags to keep them from
freezing.

Here, in the comforting dark,
the washer
rocks on its uneven floorboard,
a convulsed and
bulky tap dancer.

And I remember

coming home in the rain,
a cab's windshield wipers
lulling me to sleep,

my eyelashes turned to stone.

Fish Story

No one got away.
On the left wrist of my shirtsleeve
some blood still glistened.
Off body, the dime-sized scales of a carp
were as clear, as transparent
as windows.

And who could have seen to the stars?
I traced the bodies
of fish in the dark,
drew an enormous carp with my eye—

mustachioed, thick-lipped,
an immigrant not knowing the language,

a man lost on the streets of his
own annihilated past.

And who could have seen to the stars?
There were clay pots full of tulips.
There were cats who pawed the moon,
knocking it around like a mouse
across a marble floor.

There was a single gong
that rang and rang from the universe of
a peacock's unfurled tail.

And all this, too, was a carp:

bottom-feeder, shit eater,
a fin moving over the face of the courtesan,
a slow ghost rising to the
bowed heads of emperors—

bottom-feeder, shit eater,
how shall I forget you?

How make the story cleaner?
All the lies of purity and fate...

In the river, nudging a beer can
with your barbells,
you stay where the roots go deep,
wherever the heart has forgotten its filth—

you stay and you remember,
until, seeking a trout or a bass,

we haul you up
and curse—trash fish,
full of mud and bones,
something only the poorest
would eat.

At the My Fair Lady Lounge

An old man tells me about Cuba.
Drunk, he talks of dice
and mangoes,
half his words slurred,
the other half accented to mere guess.

A go-go dancer saunters over.
I watch him eye her breasts,
as if they could speak,
as if they were on the verge.

His hand trembles
and he puts a dollar bill
between them.
The dancer squeezes his hand
into her cleavage.

The old man smiles
mouth full of random teeth,
like rotted pier pilings.
Bonita, he murmurs.
The dancer pouts,
walks off towards a dollar bill.

The old man's crying now—
fedora gone askew on his head.
He resumes Cuba,
the mangoes and the dice.
In his mind, bone fish root
through the sand flats
of sheltered lagoons,
their bodies transparent
mirrors for the sea.

I Wish Yawl Bluebirds

That's what she said
the night they fired her,

and it was probably the same
at every diner.

Bluebirds, she said. *I wish yawl bluebirds.*

Her personality was not conducive to tips.

She had a kid,
and no husband,
and no bad habits,
just a set jaw that implied
she was living life on protest.

There were no dyke girlfriends either.

And where were the husbands,
and the dyke girlfriends?

And what did she live on?

Her daughter was no prize,
scrawny, like her, all of ten,
and with brown mustard-colored eyes
and deadpan stare
could pinch the balls of Santa.

They had no history,
and so we made it up.

That night, she said, *I wish yawl bluebirds,*
and took off
God knows where.

Down road
past the abandoned paint factory,
and the Ukrainian Catholic church
with its gold onion dome,

and the lone blood sausage hanging
in Bednarz's meat shop window.

And no one ever saw her again,
or cared,
except tonight,
for no good reason,
I remember
this old Four Season's song,
"Dawn, Go Away,"

and how she stood on her break,
between the kitchen entrance
and the cake counter,

eyes closed, arms folded, dancing,
until she saw me
and she stopped.

After Revisiting the Neighborhood

I stood there, in the late afternoon sun,
watching a little kid with a Popsicle stick
attempt to pry a penny loose from the street.

The tar was so soft. It was 92 degrees
in the middle of April.
I marveled at the kid's tenacity,
the way he remained poised
in his catcher's crouch,
digging, and probing, intent
like a chimp using a stick
to pry up some juicy ants.

A little girl in a sweater
much too warm for the weather
played hopscotch a few yards away,
tossed a black shoe heel onto the seven,
hopping, a robin, then turning back,
seemingly unaware of the boy
until he succeeded.
Then she approached with
her left hand stuck out
in the ancient gesture of *give me,*
and he did, without hesitation or protest,
and she put it in her pocket and skipped away.

An old man, squatting at ease, on his
front stoop
called to me: *Hey Red! This ain't the right weather for spring.*
You ever been to Arizona?
No sir, I said.
And he said: *Dry heat there. Not*
this sticky stuff,
dry heat—like a kiln. And he said nothing more.

The afternoon dozed on, the wild crayon-yellow forsythia
wilting, the lilacs just about to bloom, the bees premature.
When the little girl and the boy went
in for supper,
I took the shoe heel and tossed
it for good luck
into the dusk, onto the honeyed tar.

Then evening came, and I stared
at the house we had lost, remembered
the neighbors watching
as we shoved the piano onto a
friend's pickup truck, and my father said:
Get in the back and play it. Play it
for those nosey bastards!
And I played the "Boogie Woogie,"
and the tears burned through my anger.

I remembered and I watched
the spiders wake
to weave their webs from porch light to pillar post.
Lost in my act of witness, I felt
the sadness crawl away,
and thought of the boy with his stick, so single-minded,
and how far and for what he must dig.

Mr. Danish and the Butterflies

In my neighborhood, there were no kitchens
done in Southwest motif,
no Tibetan prayer wheels,
no posters of bleached skulls
by Georgia O'Keeffe.

The best jobs were tool maker,
legal secretary,
cop,
or maybe you lucked out
and got into General Motors,
and worked there the rest of your life
like Mr. Danish,
who traded in his blue Chevy
with white interior
every other year
for a blue Chevy with white interior.

Mr. Danish admired Vic Damone.
I remember him standing, shirtless, on his backyard patio,
orange shorts and lilac socks,
conducting the violins with a greasy spatula,
dancing the cha-cha with his
own enormous beer belly,
to the tune of "April Love."
His unhappy wife hissing: *Sit down. Fool.*

He died when I was seventeen,
his liver turned to mush,
his son Abby, killed in Nam,
his daughter Terry, married
to a black guy from Duluth
who sold plumbing supplies.

I would like to pretend
Terry was a courageous trailblazer

of racial tolerance,
but she was just this lumpy white girl
who squinted a lot and listened
to the Dave Clark Five.

And I am not middle-class enough, or
white liberal enough,
to think the black guy was any
great shakes, either.

He was skinny
and bewildered looking,
and talked with a high, lispy voice
that made Mr. Leo up the street
refer to them as the ugly version
of *Guess Who's Coming to Dinner.*

No one was a hero on my street,
not even Tommy Byrnes, winner
of the Silver Star,
who'd been Thorazined back into
civilian life
minus the ability to work,
whose wife, Beatrice, was pretty and cheerful
and good with flowers and, who, according
to certain sources, was balling Mr. Danish
for the occasional mortgage payment.

I kept trying to picture Mr. Danish naked
with Mrs. Byrnes,
and it depressed me.

If I was middle-class enough,
or white enough,
I could make a hero, or at least,
a victim out of her,

but she was just this pretty lady
who looked like Lee Remick,
and tipped well on the paper route.

And who knows?
Maybe she really liked Mr. Danish.
Maybe she saw something in him
no one else did, some quality
of light, some tenderness
beyond his black hair.

Maybe suffering
drew them together
for nights in cheap motels
out on 1 and 9,
a transistor radio
next to a bucket of ice,
Johnny Mathis singing
"The Twelfth of Never."
Who knows?
Weirder things have happened.
Maybe Mr. Danish
wasn't all that bad.
I remember him buying me
a cherry ice once,
when his family was out food shopping,

sitting me down on his front porch,
and him just slightly drunk, the way
all our fathers were, telling me
how he'd come from Pennsy in '49,
how he'd watched his father
die of black lung,
a great big oaf of a man whittled down
to 90 pounds,
and how the sheriff came to post their house,

and he drove here
with his brothers to Jersey,
looking for work in the asbestos plant
down in Manville,
but lucked out and got into GM,
where he'd worked ever since.

And, in spite of black lung and sheriffs,
wasn't this a goddamned beautiful country?

Where else would a guy with an
eighth-grade education,
and no past worth a whore's spit,
end up with a new Chevy and a gas grill,
and a bungalow down the shore?

And he drank another Pabst,
and told me about Ted Williams's
miraculous eye,
and Lou Gehrig's final speech,
and the Holy Shroud of Turin,
and this one field in Mexico
where all the monarch butterflies
went to spend the winter.

And, one year, he heard, they were so thick,
they made that field
look like a shield of stained glass.
Someday, he was going there,
he swore, to say a prayer for his father.

And then, he got on the subject
of Eleanor Roosevelt and how
he thought she was a classy broad,
and, if given the choice between her and

Veronica Lake, he'd have taken Eleanor,
because, he said, you go to bed
with a woman's body but you
wake up with her mind.
And you could tell he thought this
saying was wise,
because he repeated it under his breath
and looked up at the moon
as if it might agree.
And then he shut up and I noticed
he was crying.

So maybe that's what Mrs. Byrnes
saw in him.
Who knows?

The night they took his corpse out
of the house,
I remember the neighbors staring
and how his belly rose
under the white sheet.

He's been dead over twenty years now.

The jobs at GM disappeared.
Simmons and Singer went belly up.
Cancer picked off the neighbors one by one.
No one talks about
how cheap the heroin's become
on the streets of Elizabeth.

Tonight I dream the dead are balloons,
and I hold them by strings
and stand in some park,
trying to sell them to the yuppies
who pelt me with the complete works

of Victor Hugo.
I see Mr. Danish bumping up against
his murdered son,
see his face on a balloon
riffling in the wind,
and I hoist him down
and I tell him:
Listen, Mr. Danish, Johnny Mathis sucks,
but I'm taking you to that field.

And off we float above the frame houses
of my childhood,
Mr. Danish and all the host of the dead
out over the Atlantic seaboard.
And it's midnight and someone
on a radio says: *You are listening*
to the voice of the BBC.

And they play an old recording
of Pablo Casals performing
Bach's cello suites.
And all the neighborhood is there.

We land in the field where
the monarch butterflies go.
And we pray.
We pray for the living and the dead,
and I wake up praying,
and put on my work uniform,
and go to my shift factory job
where I write this poem.

An Evil Talent

Drunk, I can remember nothing except
the phone numbers of ex-lovers.
Some of them now have husbands,
others children,
soon, no doubt, they'll have grandchildren.

For some reason known only to the god of bad luck,
their numbers never change.

I say things, sometimes I say things;
most often, I just hang up.

It is enough to pour the salt in the wound,
to bite down on the abscess tooth,
to admit that I am unholy, and drunk, and searching the
connected world
for my various disconnections.
What do I need to forget to remember?
What merciful god might destroy
the proper brain cells?
I was never good at math.
What is this evil talent?

A friend suggests I store them in my cell,
and leave it at home when I'm drinking.
This seems too pedestrian a cure,
and I like that it's cold,
and the moon just went
behind the Hess station
and it's three a.m.,
and I've turned into a bad Tom Waits song.

If they only knew how much
I still loved them,
if only they would drop
everything they were doing,

including their husbands, and
come to rescue me
from whatever well I'm dropped into,
if only they cried down the
well of my longing:

Joseph come home! Here's
the long memory of our hair! Ascend!

But the conversation is over,
it was over twenty, and ten, and
five years ago.
The last word escaped out the window
like a jewel thief,
and took my record collection with it.

I am always stunned by the failure of love,
even the tenth time, the fiftieth time,
that anything that included me
and someone else
naked and reasonably happy, could end.

I am fond of my losses.
They are the children
I will never have.
I gather them up like a
copse of blue flowers.
I take them to boring lectures,
parade them through the streets.

It must be a duty of sorts.
Something I'll keep doing
until I get it right,

once every few years,
twice when the year's been bad,

I punch in a number, my heart beating,
suddenly sober, suddenly frightened,
suddenly stupid,
and pray, this time, I have it wrong.

The Sea Is Glass

The sea is glass, she says.
She points to it with a sweet potato fry.
The sea is calm.
A little boat putt-putts across the water.
She is eating my fries. She finished hers.
She talks, whether I listen or not.
She is happy in her voice.
Her laughter is loud, rowdy, obscene
in a holy sort of way.
I think how sad it is that we can't kiss
somebody's voice.
I love her voice. I love her appetite.
I want the boat to putt-putt forever.
Its wake is a perfect *V;* so is her cleavage.
There is a shadow there
without which her breasts
would have no shape.
She keeps pushing the strap of her halter top
back over her brown shoulder.
Every time she eats a fry, she pins her
still-wet hair to her spangled ear.
Her foot is lightly touching mine under the
table. She is not aware of this touching.
Perhaps she is. I am more aware of it
than I ought.
I am more aware of it than the sea.
The sea is glass. It could break.
When she moves her foot, a sadness
comes over me like summer ending.
She does not know why I am sad.
She does not care.
She finishes my fries. Surveys dessert.
Her teeth are so white in contrast to her skin.
She has eyes the color of green bottle glass.
I am in love. I am in agony.
Her left hand rests on the cafe table.

I want to touch it—her hand, or knee or thigh,
or voice, or
the shadow that shapes her breasts.
She is happy in our friendship.
I wonder if the men she fucks
know how powerfully careless she is.
Is she careless with them?
How many have kissed her tan line?
I want to go home. Now.
I want to take her halter top off.
I want to make her drop that
sweet potato fry, without regret.
I want her to eat me down to the
designer polo shirt I wear only
when we are having one of our lunches.
I want her mouth on my neck.
My neck is lonely. My throat tightens.
My hand knocks over a glass
of over-priced merlot. All over the table.
Good. This is good. I ask for the check.

Cinderella in Middle Age

In middle age, at the midpoint
of life's journey,
Cinderella finally gets the decoder ring,
two-thirds of the way through
her daughter's Cracker Jack box,
and, thereby, enters the dark
wood of her bliss.
Ah, to steal your child's prize, especially since the kid will
never know,
is a joy, certainly of a different
order, yet no less poignant
than that long-ago perfect fit.

Her stepsisters have become presidents of
the *Victims of Cautionary
Tales Support Group.*
Her stepmother is dying
slowly of emphysema.
Her prince wants her to call him
dirty names in German,
to smack his ass with a rider's crop.
No one ever informed her
that success has a different, yet no less
powerful aftertaste: boredom, boredom
in the spiked domination collar,
in the four hundred shopping sprees.

In the middle of the afternoon, at the
midpoint of life's journey,
between *All My Children*
and *General hospital,* in that terrible
lull that is *One Life to Live,*
she takes out her silver, ruby-encrusted flask.

Ah, the whiskey still burns, like poverty, like hope!
The line between humility and

humiliation is not so finely drawn.
She has returned to school for an MFA,
and is in love with
her workshop leader's ears.
Meanwhile, she does the best
she can with happily ever after,
knowing full well that, whatever it is,
it will never be enough.

The Light Above a City

Rilke would have made it
some sort of spiritual renunciation.
Dashiell Hammet would have preferred
you brought a blonde with you,
and let the cigarette dangle cynically,
as her heel caught on the cliff edge.

As for me, I have been here too many times,
expecting nothing to return.
There is no light above me
except the silver glint of a jet,
catching the sun as it banks
towards Newark.
There's an early crescent moon.
June, 7 p.m.,
two hours before the dark will make
this valley city sparkle.
The smog has lifted.
In the distance, I can hear little children
screaming to each other,
a turkey vulture
soars on the liquid air,
killing time in lieu of any roadkill.

I am sad. It is
one of those moments
when I can remember being nothing else.

A green grief for nothing in particular
grows in me—
not for the lost loves, or the missed chances,
or the loneliness of being.
Forget all that.
Leave that to the other writers.
The wind rifles through what's
left of my hair.

I kick a stone off the cliff wall.
My baggy dress shirt rustles
like a parachute.
I want to jump, but I don't.

What I'm Waiting For

What I'm waiting for is Susan Sarandon.
She can bring Tim Robbins if she wants to
I liked him in
the *The Shawshank Redemption.*
He was good in *Bull Durham.*
Very good.
Susan Sarandon certainly thought so,
but I'd prefer her alone.

I want her to arrive in late November,
while I'm sitting in a bar,
a double Jameson before me,
and only two dollars left in my pocket.

She would say: *So, what do you*
think of the French Revolution?
as she slides onto the stool beside me,
her light green dress cut on the bias,
her red hair like the soft
glow of a cigarette from
a dark porch in winter.

And I would say:
I try not to think of the French Revolution.
I don't want to lose my head.
Has anyone ever told you
you are like the soft glow of a cigarette
from a dark porch in winter?

Yes, she would say, then assuring me
originality is not her chief interest,
she would lean in, and kiss me once,
briefly but fully, and without any tongue.
She would say:
You're left-wing. I can tell. You have
a true commitment

to the end of war in the Middle East.
I can tell by the way you kiss.
Kissing me again, she'd whisper:
Help me bring justice to Hollywood.

Of course, I would.
I would do anything for Susan Sarandon.
I would go to my closet
and pull out my mask of Che Guevara.
I would march through Beverly Hills,
singing songs about the Wobblies.

I'd even buy a CD of Joan Baez,
if she insisted,
and spend all night wooing her
in the back of the protest rally.
But right now, I need a drink.

Susan, do you have any money?
I am three dollars short of Valhalla.
Sure, she says, *sure,*
and, lifting up my trouser leg

with one dainty and silk-stockinged foot,
she pulls down my black crew sock with her
pedicured toes and
tells the barkeep to bring us the bottle.

Why Is it Sometimes Loneliness...

Why is it sometimes loneliness
almost gives me character,
something beyond pity, beyond the
all-too-encompassing rapture with
my own self?

It has made me look long at the birds.
I have counted the slate-grey juncos,
noted the tit mouse building its nest
in the thorns of the campus locust.

As a child, the only thing
I was good at was staring,
often for hours at a time.
I would watch the way light
poured through a line of wet bedsheets.
I would watch the troubled weather
of my mother's face
as she hauled the sheets in.

Today, at the workshop, tired,
over-caffeinated,
I am lonely. The few words
exchanged with students
clumsy and peripheral.
How badly I want what Rumi called
"The conversation of a thousand years."
How much I would give
to stop being phony.

No one believes I am shy.
I would tell them if they asked,
how the flutter of words
that comes from my mouth
is like that starling I saw when I was 13.
One of its wings was broken.

Light caught the oily rainbow of its plumage.
It kept beating that wing against the ground
as if to wake it,
as if panic alone could heal.

These are my words—this manic wit,
that trips and prats as much
as it ever dances.

Return me, Christ, to the silence
of my own stare.
Give me one sparrow to look at, return me to
my eyes, where nothing was false,
nothing forgotten—one sentence I can speak
beyond all the lies I tell.

Things Could Be Worse

After your angelic and beautiful
and vain grandmother escapes from assisted living
in a pair of three-inch Jimmy Choos
and trips at the curb
and is sucked into the whirling brushes
of an oncoming street cleaner (bright yellow, they are always
bright yellow)
a "friend" pats you tentatively on your back
(shorthand affection for a busy age)
and says: things could be worse.

You want to prove this friend correct
by slashing her throat with a serrated bread knife.
This comfort that does not comfort,
the wisdom that is not wise,
the hidden message being always:
"Shut up already and, please, get on with it...."
How will it be endured?

Rilke understood that we carry our grief
like a portable winter,
that our jokes contain sorrows so vast
we are no longer aware of them.
Loss becomes the landscape, our bridges and malls,
the obscenity of the normal, and that last frail smudge of light
left on high windows of buildings at dusk—
why should that matter?
Whoever stops for pain?
Yet nothing that has not been
honeyed and salted
with loss is ever real.

One of her fashionable high heels lies
on a manhole cover,
the other still attached to her twisted foot.
To what odd dignity did she aspire?

The sun was bright, bright yellow,
and the young men always grew shy or overly brave in her presence.
Some hung their shaggy heads as if to lay horns in her lap,
still others capered about,
performed their most elaborate courtship dances.

And where was she walking in
the bright yellow sun?
And was her odd, freakish death,
her comic demise
so much more vulgar than the million DNRs, than
the bored grandchildren, the basic business of death?

Things could be worse, the uncomfortable comforters say,
and beyond their smugness, their secret joy that it's not them,
you know. It could be worse.
God praise her vanity,
and the high-heeled strut,
the beautiful misstep of her life.

What Part of the River Are You

for Renee Conway

She would ask questions
like *What part of the river are you?*

Then flick her cigarette
ash
and expect an answer.

I said I was the slow alluvial plane,
that part where the mud carried

swamp and egret,
catfish and muskrat.

Heavy.

She said she was
the mountain stream,
flowing quick,
a bit of speckled light
on the rocks,
rapid and shallow

where brook trout
rose.
A sound in the heart as of
rushing waters.

We were both full of shit,
fifteen and bored,
and no one really liked us.

So we hung out
talking about rivers.

I don't think you're alluvial!, she said,
long after we had left all rivers behind.
I mean, I don't see you as alluvial at all.

The stars rose over
the car we sat on—her father's decrepit Datsun.

The night filled up
with crickets, the moaning
of cats in heat,
a jet plane throbbing overhead.

Close your eyes, she said.
Close your eyes.
And when I did,
she took my hand and
softly, reverently
kissed each knuckle.

I never asked why.
She never explained.

We've been friends for thirty years.

Sometimes, I call her up, long-distance,
out west,
in Cañon City,
home of twenty private prisons,
where she lives with
her prison guard husband,
two dogs and three cats.
I call whenever I need to touch
the web of my life.

Whenever I am low or lonely
and remember her lips
on the hard bones of my hand.

In Gratitude to a God Who Is at Least As Merciful As Chekhov

I can handle God in short, dramatic doses
I could probably get down
on my hands and knees
and wash Christ's feet with my tears
and dry them with my hair (had I hair)

but could I do my laundry
every week
faithfully
and with attention to detail?
Could I clean my room,
refrain from giving
God the middle finger
when one of those calamitous failures,
to which I am heir and
for which I am usually
responsible,
occurs?

Lord, you know I'm
no long-distance runner.
The daily doings of a life,
the one right deed at a time,
the plodding, honest,
hourly practice of virtue
is beyond me.

I'm more the good thief,
the whore who
in some catastrophic hour,
by some fierce epiphany of grace
embraces you.

And so this is my poem of thanks,
thanks that you have open heaven

even to a schlepper like me,
miserable, as I am,
lonely, and horny and unable
to keep my lover or to match my socks,
that you have somehow made room
in your kingdom
for the halt and the lame,
for all those who have trouble
tying their shoes.

At least I hope so.
I hope you are as merciful as Chekhov
who knew how sorrow wrinkles the pants,
how failure unknots the tie.
Forgive me Lord for my venality,

for my heart like a box
of broken watches.
Love me, for I am so unworthy.
I have broken the jar of my life
and have begun to pour.

Poem for a Thin-Lipped Woman

There are people I'd die for,
and for no good reason,

except perhaps because the light broke
like a two-by-four
across their laps,

or because they, too, understood
the blue jay and its cry,

or sang to themselves in the middle
of closets,

or had nothing to offer me
except a real and abiding
delight in my presence.

There are people I'd die for,
hardly any of whom I have
a claim on, neither neighbor nor enemy,
spouse or lover, daughter nor son,

but random, random
as the milkweed spores
that halo my sun-dazzled head,
here in this field where I think
I might die for the weeds,
for the vintage Fresca can I nudge with my shoe,
for that old springer spaniel over there,
who is leaping in the sun, like a Pentecostal
snatching the gold mile weed spores between his teeth.

O dog maw, like a hundred wet wallets,
I'd die for you!
And for the spongy grass under my feet,
three hours removed from thaw,

and for the raindrops on these swings,
and for my wet ass.
I'd die, or live with a complete attention,
which is the same damned thing.

O death to my own importance,
and to myself 'esteem,'
and to the dirty doing of things, the 'busy'
life where life never really gets lived.

And I'd die for the thin-lipped woman,
the one who kissed me, when I didn't deserve it,
at a reading where I was drunk
and unhappy
and cracking jokes that made the whole room laugh,
and she kissed me, and I'd die for her,
she whom I crown with the milkweed spores,
and with the pale sun's diadem.

Ode to Elizabeth

"Grimy Elizabeth," *Time* magazine intones.
This city escaped the race riots,
never quite sank,
and, consequently, never rose.

It's not a town for poets,
you live here,
you work the factory or a trade.
Down the burg, in Peterstown,
Italian bricklayers sit
on stoops, boxes, chairs,
playing poker
into one a.m.

Drive up Elizabeth Avenue
and you'll hear the salsa music blast
from every window.
Even the potted geraniums dance.
In La Palmita, old Cuban guys sip coffee
from little plastic cups.
They talk politics, prizefights, Castro,
soccer, soccer, soccer.

Our mayor looks like a lesser Mayor Daley;
smokes cigars, wears loud plaid suits,
the penultimate used car salesman.
He's been in since '64, a Mick
with a machine.
He's been reelected because
he's a consistent evil
and here in Elizabeth, we appreciate consistency.

Half the law of life is hanging out,
hanging on
to frame houses, pensions.
Every Sunday, ethnic radio:

Irish hour, Polish hour,
Lithuanian hour. My father
sits in the kitchen
listening to Kevin Barry.
He wishes he could still sing.
Two years ago, they cut his voice box out:
cigarettes, factory, thirty years' worth
double shifts.
My fathers as grimy as Elizabeth,
as sentimental, crude.
He boxed in the Navy, bantamweight.
As a kid I'd beg him to pop a muscle
and show off his tattoo.

We are not the salt of the earth.
I've got no John Steinbeck illusions.
I know the people I love have bad taste
in furniture. They are likely to buy
crushed-velvet portraits of Elvis Presley
and hang them next to the Pope.
They fill their lives with consumer goods,
leave the plastic covering on sofas
and watch *Let's Make a Deal.*

They are always dreaming
the lottery number
that almost wins.

They are staunch Democrats who
voted for Reagan.
They are closing, laid off when
Singer's closed,
stuck between chemical dumps and oil
refineries in a city
where Alexander Hamilton
once went to school.

In the graveyard by the courthouse,
lie Caldwells, Ogdens, Boudinots.
Milton is quoted on their graves.
Winos sleep there on summer afternoons
under hundred-year-old elms,
they sleep on the slabs of
our Founding Fathers
and snore for history.

I have no illusions. We belong:
the winos, the immigrants, the prospering
Portuguese with their sweet-looking daughters
marching off to school and leaving
their parents'
broken English behind.

The Irish of Kerry Head have vanished,
but up in Elmora, you still can see
the Jewish families walking
home from synagogue.
They are devout, they are well dressed,
they read the Talmud.
They are not full of shit.

Twelve years ago, I used to go
to the Elmora Theater
with twenty other kids.
It was a rundown movie house that never
got the features 'til they'd been out a year.
Because the Elmora was poor, it showed
foreign films; art films we didn't
even know were art:
Fellini, Wertmüller, Bergman.
It cost a dollar to get in.

We'd sit there, factory workers' kids,
half hoods,

watching *Amarcord,* while in the suburbs
they played all the other shit.
When the grandfather climbed the tree
on *Amarcord* and screamed,
"I want a woman!"
We all agreed.

For weeks, Anthony Bravo went
around school screaming, "I want a woman!"
every chance he got.
I copped my first feel there,
saw *Hester Street, The Seduction of Mimi.*

Once they had a double feature:
Bruce Lee's *Fists of Fury*
Ingmar Bergman's
The Seventh Seal.

I remember, two hundred kids exploding
when Jack Nicholson choked the nurse
in *Cuckoo's Nest.*
Sal Rotolo stood up,
tears streaming down his face,
and when they took Jack's soul away,
we all sat there silent.
It lingered with us all the way home,
empty-eyed and sad.

Here in Elizabeth, tasteless city,
where *Amarcord* was allowed
to be just another flick,
where no one looked for symbols,
or sat politely through the credits.
If Art moved us at all,
it was with real amazement;
we had no frame of reference.

And so I still live here,
because I need a place where
poets are not expected.
I would go nuts
in a town where everyone read Pound,
where old ladies never swept their stoops
or poured hot water on the ants.

I am happiest in a motley scene,
stuck between Exxon and the Arthur Kill…
I don't think Manhattan needs another poet.
I don't think Maine could use me.
I'm short, I'm ugly,
I prefer Mrs. Paul's Fish Sticks
to blackened redfish.
I don't like to travel because I've noticed
no matter where you go,
you take yourself with you,
and
that's the only thing I care to leave behind.

So I stay here.
At night, I can still hear mothers yelling,
"Michael, supper! Get your ass in gear!"

Where nothing is sacred,
everything is sacred.
Where no one writes, the air seems strangely
charged with metaphor.

In short, I like a grimy city.
I suspect culture
because it has been given over
to grants, credentials, and people
with cute haircuts.
I suspect poetry because it talks to itself

too much, tells an inside joke.
It has forgotten how to pray.
It has forgotten how to praise.

Tonight, I write no poem. I write to praise.
I praise the motley city of my birth.
I write
to be a citizen of Elizabeth, New Jersey.
Like a goddamned ancient Greek,
I stand for this smallest
bit of ground, my turf, this squalid city.
Here, in the armpit of the beast.

Tonight, the ghosts of Ogdens, Caldwells, Boudinots walk
among the winos.
They exist in the salsa music
blaring on Elizabeth Avenue.
They rise up and kiss the gargoyles
of Cherry Street.
They are like King David dancing naked
unashamed before the covenant.

Tonight even the stones can praise.
The Irish dead of Kerry Head are
singing in their sleep.
And I swear the next time someone makes
a face, gives me that bit-the-lemon look,
as if to say, *My Gawd...How can you be a poet and live in that
stinking town?*
My answer will be swift.
I'll kick him in the balls.

from **Painting the Christmas Trees**

The First Time I Got Up Early

The first time I got up early,
and put my work boots on
and knew that they meant work,
I was nineteen, freshly dropped out of college,
and I came downstairs to join my father
in the kitchen.
He'd lost his larynx the year before,
had learned to belch out words without a voice box.
He stood there in his white Stone Products uniform,
and I stood there in my work boots,
and he just cried. His stoma, the hole
they leave you with when they cut a larynx out,
filled up with mucus. He had to dab it with a tissue.
He said nothing, but pulled two soft bills from his wallet
and handed them to me.

Later, when I came home, machine grease in my pores,
stinking of coolant mist and sweat,
he offered me a beer. "Here, kid," he belched—
my father, fifty-five years old, reduced
from Grade A Machinist to janitor, the guy who cleaned the toilets,
cancered, and canceled. He said, "Work is work…
only the bosses get to call it a career."
We sat for an hour on the porch, letting the tiredness drink
us, the warm night touch us with its fur. He said, "I'm sorry."
I said, "What are you sorry for?" He didn't answer,
just opened another beer. I wanted to kiss him, but I didn't.
There were these blanks between us, as beautiful
and hopeless as the sky. There were these blanks.
And what could we have filled them with?
Later, when he was too drunk to walk, I helped him up the stairs,
took his work shoes off, cleaned the snot from his throat hole,
covered him with a blanket. This was love. I meant it,
silent, and knowing it could kill me. I took my time.

Elegy for Sue Rapeezi

She was the kind of girl who never
took her ugliness lying down.
Once, Jimmy Tarantino
called her a titless bitch
and she waited 'til he turned his head
then hit him with a four-foot length
of plumber's pipe.

Some claimed she was a dyke,
others a whore,
still others a dick-tease.
(Sue was a triple threat.)

The other girls didn't like her.
She had a rapport with silence,
a rawboned gentleness
the world does not permit.

For unknown reasons
she took a liking to me,
came calling at my house
though I did my best to avoid her:
helped my mother with the laundry,
helped my father fix his brakes.

I was fourteen then and a closet intellectual
who kept Schubert piano sonatas
hidden inside Led Zeppelin album covers.

She caught me listening to Schubert.
She didn't put me down.
I lived in mortal fear
of losing my cool.

I thought it was my destiny
to carry Schubert as a secret

through all the beer-guzzling contests
and acts of hard-guy bravado.

"What's that shit?" she asked.
"Schubert," I replied.
"I like it," she said. "Sounds sad."

After a while, I let her come upstairs—
this ugly girl with dirty fingernails.
She'd sit through Schubert, Mozart,
even Bach.
"When I die," she said, "I hope they play that shit...
I mean, if they play 'Kumbaya' or
some other asshole song, I swear,
I'll haunt the motherfuckers...."

I decided she was cool,
sort of Edith Piaf
without talent.
One day, she asked me
if I'd ever considered
fucking her brains out.
"No," I said. "The thought
never crossed my mind."

"You know," she said, "you could
if you wanted to."
I said no thanks.
She said, "Stuck-up faggot."
And walked out.

Weeks passed.
I was listening to Wagner.
I started wishing she was there,
sitting on my bed, eyes closed-ears open,
someone to share the sound with.

So I went down to the deserted train station
where she often sat
reading her vampire novels
and I asked her to come back.

We made love in the attic.
I had never felt a naked body
besides my own.
It felt good.
As flat as she was, I learned the noun
and verb of a woman's body
are not always in agreement,
that an "ugly" girl
could be beautiful in motion.
She was graceful, warm, she didn't cause me grief.

After that, we sort of just hung out,
listening to Wagner,
getting wasted on quarts of Schaefer beer.
Her father got a job down south.
She moved away.
Ten years went by.

Last week, I saw her name in the obituaries.
She'd moved back up to Elizabeth,
and was killed on the Parkway,
rolled over in a van.
She wasn't drunk,
just unlucky.

Excuse me, God,
but I feel this woman is an imposter.
The photo showed a different face
from the one I knew.
I feel they've usurped my old friend's name,
but, if it's true,

I pray they carried her away to Mozart.
There's so little in this life we own.
I pray in the end
she was saved
from bad music.

Variations on a Theme by Isaiah

I ride my bike past a deserted house on Burnett Street.
A premature moon rises over the Chivas Regal sign.
A child, maybe nine, who has written on the sidewalk
"THE ROCK" in bold rainbow-colored chalk,
is busy giving me the finger.
I give him the finger too.
I feel the muscles tighten in my legs.
The wind opens and shuts a broken screen door—
a distillation of the neighborhood's futility.

As I pass, the kid whacks me in the back with a dirt bomb.
I turn to glare, and the white blossoms of a catalpa
drop petals all over the little bastard.
He is like a god standing there, transfigured,
his whole being lost in the flowers.
He is laughing like a god.
He, no doubt, tortures bugs.
His father is probably missing an arm
and shows up once a week with an assault rifle
to take him to piano lessons.

"Faggot," says the kid.
"Lucifer," says I.
"The Rock's a wussy," I continue.
I, too, grew up in this neighborhood,
know its cheerful hostilities,
its wiseass ways.
After a few hard stares, I take off down the road
and realize I am happy.
I like the way the sun stripes my T,
like the way the catalpa blossoms fall,
blazing with light, all over that kid,
so that the divine and godly show
no sense of deservedness whatsoever,
but only this hour and this hymn.
God bless that angry little shit.
God bless this angry little shit.
This, too, is a poem of praise.

The Great Grandmother Light

The Great Grandmother light,
the light that transfigures
onion skins
left on a pantry floor,

the memory of friends...

what is it that makes you lean
into this winter's night?

Suppose it's not Vermeer
but something else:

only a few dead leaves,
tumbling over the blacktop,
as you stand,
watching your father work on the car.

He tells you to keep your mind
on the job, stop wiggling the flashlight,

but the leaves swirl in ever-tighter circles,
little cyclones of dead leaves
and you're only ten and already you feel
cut off at the stem,
set adrift in the dusk
where your father bends over the car
five years removed from his death.

The Great Grandmother light
falls from windows
just before dark,
when you come home from playing hoop,
lungs feeling a sweet burn, face
flushed and dirty. The Angelus rings
and you enjoy your life,

enjoy the strange hunter's bliss
of coming home.

The Great Grandmother light
yields to the broken boards
of deserted houses,
falls into and sweetens
the black coffee of old men
whose wrinkles still contain
the cinders of coal mines.

The Great Grandmother light
is singing in her sleep, filthy and homeless,
the songs of a lost tribe.

From My Elizabeth

It's praise we enter—
This thin gruel of stars
Above the Chinese takeout,

Or the leaf rot
Smell of cold night's air—

What all begins
My journey into things:

Dogs, front yards, trees,
The rain-sodden acorn
That drops
A hundred feet
To ring the hood of a van,

A kid drags a stick
Along a broken chain-link fence,
Loving the top hat sound of steel mesh
Enough to wager his life
Against six lanes of traffic.

It's winter and twenty-eight years ago.

I walk past

Moy's candy store and Bartone's bakery,
Affecting my wounded soldier limp.
Ice crystals form
In the clear ooze of my nose.

A block away, there's the hard pecking
Of a basketball

Against the uneven sidewalk,
And then

This girl
Dribbles up,

This girl in Raider's ski cap,
Who, spinning the world on her finger,
Rolling it shoulder to elbow,
Dishes a perfect cheat pass
And says: "Hi."

Weil, You Suck, or Perpetually in Right

The taste of failure has sand in it,
and there's no way to rid the mouth of grit,
and I remember loafing home after
wondering why God would send seven balls
to right.
It was God who did it.
Had to be.
Usually, a right fielder
could pick his drawers from the crack of his ass,
practice spitting between his teeth,
have a Zen experience watching
puffs of sand blow in from second base.

But no:
Seven balls,
three in one inning,
all rolling to the edge of the train tracks
after I missed them,
and Mr. Zelinger telling his son's team
to hit the ball to that lame red-haired kid
in right,
bringing all the ruthless Darwinian
exploitation of weakness to bear
down on my nine-year-old head.

Hit it to that lame red-haired kid in right!
And I remember the tears mingling with sweat
and the disgusted voices of
my teammates moaning: Weil, you suck,
and all the time spent practicing alone
in the backyard pretending I was
Roberto Clemente.
And it was only a game my mother insisted,
but she was wrong.
It was never a game.
And those who could play

lived in peace with their bodies,
and those who couldn't, found themselves
eating lunch alone in the cafeteria
praying no jock would pass
and scorn their olive loaf,
or whack them facedown into the tuna salad.

And it was God,
who seemed only a more powerful version
of Mr. Zelinger,
who did it.
God who willed seven balls to right,
who gave Denis Sauer a kidney ailment
that made her smell like rotten eggs,
who sent Tommy Griese's dad home every
night drunk up the street to stumble
and vomit in front of every cool and
unforgiving kid.
God made my body so that its nouns and verbs
were never in agreement.

So I gave God the middle finger.
I raised my finger to the sky.
Fuck God and Mr. Zelinger.
And my mother could never understand
what all the fuss was about.
And my father let blue smoke flume out of his nose
ensconced in his TV dragon chair
and insisted it was all a matter of
"growing up."
And that night I dreamed Roberto Clemente
came into my bedroom
and sat on the edge of my bed the way a TV
father would
and said: They are full of shit.
You're a wonderful human being.

And his glove smelled like love
all leathery sweet
as he placed it over my face
and put me out of my misery.

The Dead Are in My Living Room

The dead are in
my living room.
Uncle Ernie insisted he
be placed
in that toy outhouse he so loved:
you know—the one with the
little boy tinkling
with his ding-dong out?

It seems appropriate.
My uncle was an obnoxious man,
the kind of guy you see in Atlantic City
wearing a bright orange tank top,
black fur on his shoulder blades,
slapping his son in the face
in front of four thousand people,
"teaching the kid a lesson."

My mother sits in a silver urn
on top of the piano.
When I had scarlet fever,
she played "Sweet Georgia Brown"
twenty-three times for me.
Towards the end of her life,
she cut a tendon in her left wrist
washing out a beer glass
and couldn't play the bass parts anymore.
I used to watch her staring
at her bum hand
then at the piano
then at her hand again.
She had large dark eyes—like Madame Bovary—
and thin pale lips.
And I don't know why I'm telling you this.
Suffice to say—the dead are here:
Uncle Ernie, Mom, our pet dog Rex...

I am what keeps them alive.
I keep their silence
palpable.
Often I catch myself
humming "Sweet
Georgia Brown"
late at night
when no one's listening.
You think I've gone mad?
Even Uncle Ernie deserves my strict attention
for I grab him by his lapels in dreams,
shout: Stupid, Stupid, Stupid!
Until he is a child again
with my mother's large, dark eyes
and HIS FATHER is standing
over him
slapping HIS face
teaching HIM a lesson.
What are these lessons?
Fathers in orange tank tops.
Mothers with bum left hands.
I DON'T KNOW.
What is holy or memorable
or worth preserving over the whole of this earth?
I know only that the dead are in my living room.
I can't just kick them out.

For Bro

Once, Ginger Laganga caught a hundred lightning bugs,
and, squashing them into the soles of her Keds,
scuffed out my brother's name
on the sidewalk
in green lightning bug light.

Years later, she married some Greek
who owned a Sunoco station, a travel agency,
and a funeral home.
I forget his name. We called him
Alexander the Great.

I wonder how Ginger's doing.
My brother has wet brain—too many shots and beers—
his throat cut for cancer, his gut and liver swelled.
And the neighborhood's as bad off as he is.
I hope Ginger's in the Aegean,
sunning the best pair of breasts money can buy.

She really loved my brother.
I remember thinking how great
for someone to write your name in the sidewalk
like that. Never mind the more brutal
aspects of the procedure.
Love is brutal and stupid and gets you nowhere.
I ought to know.
I love my brother.

Forget the drink and the money he owes me.
He can't remember what he said five minutes ago.
His short-term memory is gone.

I want to punch God out.

God's the only thing big enough for my grief.
Outside this air-conditioned hospital,

the day's a hot brick to the face.
I'm sweating so bad, it stings my eyeballs,
trickles into the crack of my ass.

In lieu of God, I punch a wall and nearly bust my hand.
My brother's going to die, begging for a beer.

I remember him in footsies, dancing the twist.
I remember him saying: "Don't worry, I got it covered, Bro."
Johnny, there ain't enough shit in this world
to cover it.

I see Ginger Laganga scuffing out your name in the dusk.
That was over thirty years ago.
She used to stroll down the street with Patty Devlin,
singing "The Name Game," or "Chapel of Love."
They were jump rope champs
and I see the long loop of the two ropes,
and Ginger and Patty riding it out, jumping
just high enough, not even a whisper
between them and the street.

And Ginger ate a sky blue jet pop as she jumped,
licked it from all directions, eyes half-closed,
a middle finger thrust up at the law of gravity.
And Patty blew an enormous gum bubble that
grew like some scientist's model for an expanding universe.

And I am holding my nearly broken hand now
outside this hospital.

There's nothing to console me.
Last week, you asked the same question
a dozen times in an hour.

You're retarded, Bro.
Worse, you have enough intelligence left to know it.

I want to kiss the middle of your forehead
and make you well again.

Ginger Laganga, where are the gestures of dusk
when you really need them?
I see lightning bugs, hear canned TV laughter
come through a screen door.
I am growing old and fat and the sadness is winning.

I want to sing for my brother, but he's
not home anymore.
I will sing to his empty house,
the dark porch of his memory,
forgive everything and forget nothing.
This is the best I can do.

Confession

Don't speak to me of love.
I drove the sun's car and totaled it.

Ruined, light dallied with weeds,
romped through the hairs of old women,
turned rivers to bronze.

I touched those waters with my hands.
It was like fondling a new language.

And where were the verbs? And what
nouns hid like bridge trolls
to devour me?

Not understanding a word, I entered the music,
consonant and vowel, glottal and phoneme.

Rivers, forgive me.
There was a woman.
There was silence.
There was the same old
pain
wearing its business suit.

I did not go too far—
splash and wavelet,
spew and spar,
I drove the sun's car
and totaled it,
setting loose a thousand shadows,
one of which hid in the weeds

and frightened me into song.

Minnows

"So little," says the woman to the figure in the
coffin—
eight children blown to bits, their fingers flying,
flying fingers, heads, arms, legs, toys.
One man wipes the blood from his eyeglasses.
Someone takes a photo.
These murderers have no venial sins.
They pray several hours a day.
They never pick their noses.
Virtue scares me.
I am tired of just causes.
I would settle for a pretzel.
The holy is so little,
the size of a finger.
It does not understand victory.
It does not understand defeat.
I saw it once swimming with a school of minnows.
But who remembers the minnows when they are
blowing up the children?
Too many speeches,
a man with minnows on his mind,
who picks his nose,
who does not understand victory or defeat,
who makes no speeches,
where is such a man?
"So little" says the woman to the figure in the
coffin.
I am waiting for the world to notice
minnows, holiness smaller than a finger.
Only some vast silliness might save us.
This is no time to be serious.
There are children in their coffins.

This is no time for inspiration,
but the speeches will come,
each more ponderous than the other.

Truth swims with the minnows.
A man wipes his eyeglasses.
The murderers pray.
They believe in heaven.
They do not believe in earth,
though it rise to kiss their feet.
The earth is lost, lost to some idea
for which the slaughter of children is necessary.
Arms, legs, fingers go flying.
The word tragedy is brandished.
I am keeping my eyes on the minnows.
I am watching the moon.
These days of disinheritance,
we feast on human heads.
Birds rebuild old nests.
The children cannot be rebuilt.
Their fingers enclose the sun.
I refuse to see them in an afterlife.
They were of the earth.
It rose to kiss their feet.
I want an end to speeches.
"So little" says the women to the figure in the
coffin,
holiness smaller than a finger,
beyond the butchery of ideas,
beyond the murderers who pray.
I want to pick my nose.
I want to sit in the sun and watch the minnows swim.
Why does a black night gather in my mouth?
The wind has blown the silence of summer away.
The last leaf that is going to fall has fallen.
There is so much we have to un-know,
so many certainties to vanquish,
before we can even begin to live on this earth
in the full difficulty
of what it is to be.

Bay Way, Elizabeth, Six a.m., Eastern Standard Time

Early morning, Bay Way.
I walk upwind from the oil tank herds,
enter the same disquieting stillness
I remember from thirty years ago,
watching my father sleep off a double shift:

the unsteady rise and fall of his chest,
his work uniform still on, covered in paper dust,
old god monster of my childhood.

And now this neighborhood rises and falls,
its exhalations a war between smells:
honeysuckle and dog shit,
bus fumes and babka bread.

I've copped a *Times* and
a coffee regular to go.
The cup warms my hand, feels
like fresh-laundered flannel.
Who wants this day to begin?

The piano store's metal eyelid
is still closed.
Mr. Gerdung dusts the baby grand,
chases out the kids who come to touch its keys.
Their parents don't do right, he says.
Their parents don't buy pianos.
Just one accordion student left,
and he's lazy, without talent.

The wife standing next to Vladimir Horowitz
in a photograph from 1962 is dead
ten years come May—
the same dead wife, the same unsold piano.
Usually, Mr. Gerdung opens early.
I listen to his stories and he lets me play.

His words are a ritual of loss.
They have their own peculiar beauty.

Sycamore, sweet gum, swamp maple
line the streets, their roots
pushing the sidewalks up and out.
Old Polish grandmothers who scrubbed these walks
on hands and knees are dying.
Their names bloom in the obituaries,
attached to Simmons and Singer's
long-closed plants.

At the corner of Bay Way Avenue,
a bus lets out a flock of Haitian nurses,
fresh from the all night shift in the 'burbs.
Their soft laughter,
their warm, bubbling patois
is more beautiful to me than the sound of ocean waves.

Pray God such voices
surround me in my last sleep.
Lonely and happy to be alone,
here, in Bay Way, Elizabeth—
a coffee in my hand.

To a Jerry-Rigger

My father made everything work out all right,
albeit in a left-handed sort of way:
cars, marriages, door-knobs.
We had a dining room table with a bad leg he propped
up and leveled off with the 1965 *Encyclopedia Britannica.*
We had a TV from the antenna of which
he rigged ten-pound test
(twelve was too heavy, eight was too light)
and tied it to the infant of Prague
who was just at the right height
to insure Channel 4's immaculate reception.

Actually, we had two TVs:
one with no picture, one with no sound.
My father watched the Jets game, making small,
minor adjustments,
sticking his hand up the baby Jesus's dress,
adapting to the weather, the interference of
the electrical cake mixer next door.

He had shoes he patched with cardboard,
an abscessed tooth he treated with a tea bag,
one suit he sewed until it sprouted weeds,
until the knees grew too threadbare for even his
expansive sense of use.
He worked the swing shift,
came home odd hours,
missing parts of his once-impressive fingers.
He scraped, he improvised, he made things stretch
until he broke
and who was there to fix him?
What gentle, Jerry-rigging God
could have patched my father up?

What line could have held him from his dying
when I whispered: Live.
And all the world kept breaking and the sun
shone with such an immaculate contempt?

Adelino

Deep into winter when the cold
bit like a pit, locked jaw and squeezed,
Adelino'd be out there in his cutoff sleeves,
do-rag frozen in his pocket, blasting salsa,
winching engines out of Fords—
old junkers driven by the hold-on-by-the-nails
sort of customers he served.

For a bottle of Colt 45 and a dirty joke,
you could chew him down to cost.
No wonder he went broke and sold out to Perez
but worked there for the next ten years,
healer of the gut-shot trans,
king of the perpetual, "I can fix."

Adelino drank four quarts of Colt a day,
then walked to the Polish National Home
where the Poles had put salsa
on the jukebox in his honor,
and he banged shooters until the old songs came.

"Wolf songs," he called them,
not the songs on the juke but
the tunes in his head,
songs he remembered that could
pull down a man and feed on his heart.
And then Adelino would begin to sing

in the bawling, braying, plaintive voice of an ass,
lament upon lament, with enough sentiment,
enough liquor to embalm all his ancestors.
The gentle Polacks took him to his rest,
carried him, still singing, downstairs
to sleep off his jag with the cats.
And this is how Adelino lived,
performing auto-repair miracles,

subsisting on bar nuts and Slim Jims,
until the computerized systems came,
and his liver went,
and Perez the owner let him go.

He ended up doing the bartender's
tune-ups for shots and beers,
until, one night, he hot-wired
Perez's Corvette and took it up
to a hundred and twenty
into the neighborhood's biggest tree.

And lots of people intended
to go to his wake, but no one did.
Instead, they just talked about him,
the mechanical genius, the epic drunk,
the worst singer who ever lived,

bum-legged Rican,
whose life was a broken mirror,
whose hands were blessed,
whose great heart was pulled down
and consumed by wolves.

Elegy for Lady Clairol

Lady Clairol has lost
her will to live.
We all saw it coming:
the stolid gaze,
the strained look
of cheap allegory
around the eyes.
She gathers her bravery now
into one last bright bouquet
as the sun sets over
a ruined postcard shop.

Ah, lady, who could revive one hour,
save one flower
from the arc of its decay?
Your breasts sag
and your teeth drop out:
like some rose petals they fall,
and all around you—
T-shirts and lepers.
The perfume of
boredom.

Men never understood you,
mistress of Proteus as you were,
your hair changing hue,
changing shade in infinite flight
from astounded hands.
Now, may the earth grow blonde
in your memory.
May its roots weep black
and refuse to be comforted.

Painting the Christmas Trees

In my odyssey of dead-end jobs,
cursed by whatever gods
do not console,
I end up
at a place that makes
fake Christmas trees:
thousands!
Some pink, some blue,
one that revolves ever so slowly
to the strains of "Silent Night."

Sometimes, out of sheer despair,
I rev up its RPMs
and send it spinning
wildly through space—
Dorothy Hamill
disguised as a balsam fir.
I run a machine
that spits paint
onto wire boughs,
each length of bough's a different shade—
color coded—so that America will know
which end fits where.

This is spray paint of which I speak—
no ventilation, no safety masks,
lots of poor folk speaking
various broken tongues,
a guy from Poland with a ruptured disk
lifting fifty-pound boxes of
defective parts,
a Haitian
so damaged by police "interrogation"

he flinches when you
raise your arm too suddenly near,

and all of us hating the job,
knowing it's meaningless,
yet singing, cursing, telling jokes,
un-entitled to anything but joy,
the lurid, unreasonable joy
that sometimes overwhelms you
even in a hole like this.

It's a joy rulers
mistake for proof of the *Human Spirit*.
I tell you it is Kali,
the great destroyer,
her voice singing amidst butchery and hate.
It is Rachel the inconsolable,
weeping for her children.
It goes both over and under
the *Human Spirit*.
It is my father
crying in his sleep
because he works
twelve-hour shifts six days a week
and can't make rent.

It is one hundred and ten degrees
in the land of fake Christmas trees.
It is Blanca Ramirez keeling over pregnant
sans green card.
It is a nation that has
spiritualized shopping,
not knowing how many lost
to the greater good of retail.
It is Marta the packer
rubbing her crippled hands with
Lourdes water and hot chilies.
It is bad pay and worse diet and
the minds of our children
turned on the wheel of sorrow—

no language to leech it from the blood,
no words to draw it out—
a fake Christmas tree
spinning wildly in the brain,
and who can stop it, who
unless grief grows a hand
and writes the poem?

Paunch

In the middle of getting dressed,
ambushed by a mirror,
I'm brought up halt and shamed
before the paunch.
It isn't a gut or beer belly,
a spare tire or love handles,
but something sinister, something
beyond the often tender misshapenness
of me.

Suddenly, I'm not young anymore
and that twenty-five-year-old poet
who liked my work, who spoke
with a voice like dusk, who swept
waves of thick jet hair
from her shining face as she spoke,
really only liked my work.

How awful. How sad
to be entering the realm
of the fathers.
There is no hope unless it be
a twig of slippery elm,
a perfectly blue dinner plate,
a flower I don't remember ever seeing
that gives off the spice
of a woman's sun-warmed back.

Where are those magical things?
How to find them?
And if I should master the elements,
what then?

I'll still be Prospero at best,
that old bag of tricks, vengeful,
clinging to his beautiful daughter.

Sit ups are, of course, out of the question.
This goes way beyond fitness.
This is the one grey hair
I spend mornings searching for
and pluck like a fat autumn shrew
from its lair.

Fierce and merciless as an owl,
I hover over the ruins of my life.
Trying to suck the demon in, I fall
three waist lines short of Valhalla.

Christ have mercy!
Keep me far from mirrors
and voices like dusk
in which the Angelus rings
and the stars rise,
for I am only a poet, a fat poet
heartsick with desire
and fastened to a dying animal.

So Kiss Me, Asshole

The best slice of pizza I ever had
was up in Providence, Rhode Island,
in a joint whose name I don't recall,
and in which I'll probably never set foot again.

And the best kiss I ever had occurred without
me getting laid. I was twelve.
It was dusk in the neighborhood
of unhappy waitresses.
This girl with long, stringy hair, frosted lip gloss,
green eye shadow, one of those fuzzy sweaters,
was hanging upside down from the limb
of an anemic swamp maple.
She was catching flakes of March snow on her tongue.
I was passing by, dribbling a basketball.
"So kiss me, asshole," she said.

Now there were six or seven ways of saying *asshole*
on my street, three of which were, depending
on the circumstance
and inclination of the hour, terms of endearment.
Her request came so matter-of-factly from
her upside-down lips, with such candor,
that I did exactly as I was told.

Her tongue was the coldest bit of turf
on which I'd ever trespassed,
but, oh, it warmed,
and, for a full minute, she sucked my tongue,
and bit my lower lip, and gently kissed
where she had bitten.
Though blood rushed to her head, she kept
on kissing until my twelve-year-old member
made its presence known against my corduroys.

"Touch my breasts," she whispered.
And I did, gingerly, not knowing the language,
unsure of exactly how much pressure to apply.
Her sweater left tufts of cotton on my fingers.
I stared down at my palms amazed,
as March wind blew the tufts to float like
milkweed spores around us.
"Goodbye," she said, and swung upright
on a branch, then through a window,
presumably her bedroom,
where she disappeared.

I never saw her again,
except, perhaps, the ghost of her,
riding a bike on gloomy Sunday afternoons,
or poised in mute profile at a red light
in her mother's car.
It doesn't matter.
I'm not even sure where this poem is heading,
except, a really good slice of pizza,
or a kiss, can save your life,
and I believe there are moments
that mark us with an ashy thumb,
so that we are
stained for love, so that our stories
are stories only when they've been retold, a hundred times,
if only to ourselves, if only when we expect nothing,
and deserve nothing,
and, in the hidden valleys under the rose,
a voice whispers: "So kiss me, asshole."
And we do.

Fists

for my father

It was the sense that your fists were worlds
And mine were not
That caused me to worship you;
All those thick-rope veins,
And the deep inlaid grime of your life,
The permanent filth of your labors.

I wanted your history.
My own smoothness appalled me.
I wanted that hardness
Of fists.
I'd pry your fingers loose,
Using both my hands,
Find stones, a robin's egg uncrushed
In the thick meat of your palms.
Between thumb and forefinger, your flesh smelled
Of creosote and lye,
Three packs of Chesterfield Kings.
You told me stories about heroes,
David with his sling,
Samson with the jawbone of an ass,
Christ with his word *forgive.*

Tonight, I read about Cuchulain
Contending with the sea,
How he killed his son in battle,
A son he'd never known,
And, mad with his grief,
Fought the waves
For three nights and as many days,
Until, at last, he came ashore,
And fell asleep holding his dead child's hands.

When he woke, it was morning, and the hands of his son
Had become two black swans.
They flew west where all suffering ends.
I read this story
And I remember you.
Hold me clenched until I am those birds.
Sleep now,
Until your fists can open.

from **The Plumber's Apprentice**

Christmas: 1977

Here where it is always Bethlehem,
grimy, grieved—a slumlord's kind of town,
I watch old Mrs. Suarez string her lights
against the common vespers of despair.

I watch her nimbly snub the cold night's air,
thwarting a fall into the snowball bush
beside which Mary calmly stomps the skull
of Satan. Look! the Lights are coming on:

Blue with white specks, where the paint has chipped,
and yellow, green, all rising to full glow,
big gumdrop lights, draped from post to post,
haloed where their heat meets with the cold.

And something in me tears or has been torn
a long, long time, though I have read Rimbaud,
and have been known to chew on my own spleen,
and spend an evening jesting at a God.

Something in me breaks and will not mend.
Take up my broken hymn and hang it there
for Mrs. Saurez, wobbly, and infirm,
who soon will be too old to climb her chair.

For her I hang this broken Christmas hymn,
here, where it is always Bethlehem.

In the Camden Aquarium Dreaming a Woman Who Reads Dante

A woman in a light green dress
with matching handbag,
an expert on Dante who,
taking off her white gloves,
with a careful, careful nonchalance,
sits down to read the
La Vita Nuova.

I hear her as I stand
watching the fish swim
in the Camden aquarium.

Camden: gutted city
where still the sound of Italian vowels
and the silence of fish recalls

I am human. I am
falling to my death. I
am falling
deathwards, but at this
voice full of Dante
who has time to gauge the height?

So each beautiful thing is reprieve,
and stay of execution,
recompense

the face of a child
the color of apricots
so close against the glass
his fingers smudge the fish—

his mother yanks his arm,
the fish escape—

languid tails disappearing
into the dark,
one final glint of a scale—
that flashes silver, one full Italian vowel.

When I Was Twelve

When I was twelve, I spent a year staring at the back
of Maria Casarez's head, all through
history, and religion, and Math, and I never grew bored.

All my friends preferred Patty Low—the blonde with the periwinkle eyes,
and I had nothing against blondes, with periwinkle eyes,
but I wrote my first poem for Maria:

I wrote that her hair was a dark lawn at dusk,
on which old men and women played croquet,
that she was sad and wonderful—like a fingernail moon above
Blumetti's Liquors.

I read a poem in a book I stole from the library.
(Books were always better when you stole them.)
It read: "Lark of my house, laugh often."

It was by the Spanish poet, Miguel Hernández,
tubercular shepherd, whom Franco had locked up in prison.
The introduction was by Pablo Neruda.

I knew nothing of Pablo Neruda or Miguel Hernández,
knew nothing of poetry accept that Hernández's wife and son
had been starving, living on little but wild onions,

and that, from his prison cell, from his dying,
he wrote: "Lark of my house, laugh often,
so that, even dead, and whirling through space,

I might hear your laughter,
Lark of my house, laugh often and grow strong,
for you can eat the moon when you want to."

These words made me cry. I walked home past the basketball courts,
past St. Mary's cemetery, past the billboard of the Marlboro man,
and decided I was in love with Maria Caserez.

Love made me feel enormous, and frightened,
and so small all at once,
and now I knew why idiots broke into song.

in the middle of movies, why they swung from light poles,
and tap-danced on ceilings. I wanted to die for something—
or live in this intensity that had overwhelmed me so that

I suddenly noticed the stars hung in the anemic swamp maple
outside my frame house, so that this tree was now
the heaven tree of stars, and not just the pain in the ass

my father wanted to cut down,
so that now I was ready to read poems, and to live and die,
as the Lark of somebody's house.

For Jordan, a Kid from Paterson Who Visited My House

We cart rocks from the flood wall
to surround the fire,
great heaving stones that make dents in the soft earth.

These kids from a neighborhood of street gangs
are afraid of the daddy longlegs in the shower.

I swat and smush casually with my hand,
killing all bugs, showing off for the boys.

We sit down by the fire, telling ghost stories,
bragging and laughing, risk getting burned

leaping over the flames. I haven't felt
this alive in years. The older brother, Jordan,
remembers his father, a dealer who got busted

and sent up for thirteen years. I say to him:
"He must've been top of the line.

Thirteen years…Shit, that aint no punk time."
He nods: "Yeah, we had a big house—three floors."
and takes a stick to the hot coals and scrapes

until they burst into flame. He tells me his dad
smiled when he visited him in prison. His father's

getting deported to Columbia as soon as
his stretch is up. He wants to see his father again, there,
on the coast, where they ride white horses

through the foam of the sea, where every rock
has a story. His dark eyes stare at me through the flames.

There are tears massing at the borders of his eyes.
He is looking for a father anywhere. Me, too.
How fragile our bravado is. I teach him how to

bob and weave, how to cut the ring, throw
from the heel. No round house. He wants to be a boxer
and a writer. When I give him my poems,
he reads them through, long and carefully.
Says with surprise, "You don't write like a white guy."

This is my highest compliment. I know, I tell him
in my neighborhood the Cuban Grandmas

called me *El Blanco*. He picks up a marshmallow,
the last one, and offers it to his little brother.
He has valor, a good heart. What will these do for him?

A single beef, and he might catch a bullet.
The world is not particular in whom it chooses

to slaughter. His father, he says, was different.
He read books. He sang songs. He dealt dope
because he wanted that house with three floors

and no roaches—bug-free, a clean shower.
When they go, the land seems to hold them

a few hours, the way a pool empty at dusk
holds the afternoon's laughter, the sounds of
splashing, the voices of kids horsing around

until the dark drops down to silence it again.
I clean out the ash from the fire. I, too,

am an orphan upon the earth. *El Blanco,* the whitest
motherfucker in my neighborhood.
I say a prayer for him. I pray he gets those

hooves in the foam of the sea. I pray
he dodges every bullet. What the fuck?

What can a man do with a land where
every stone tells a story? Listen. Shema
lost in the busy lives we think we lead—

the mute essential poverty,
the true blood of stones and stars.

In My Neighborhood Everyone Almost Wins the Lottery

There was Mrs. Spazzola who dreamed
the moon was following her late beloved husband,
Patsy Spazzola,
on his way to his old job,
the one he'd lost before the tumor showed
and finished him off,
and she tried desperately to remember
the exact address of his old factory,
but got it wrong, and—wouldn't you know?
That was the Pick 5 number that paid a hundred thou.

And there was Jimmy the Horse, the bookie
with the sizable overbite
who, rumor had it, had won but kept
the million cash payout
under his bed which he set on fire
drunk on Johnny Walker Blue.

When the fire went out, all that was left of Jimmy
were his gold-plated cuff links, and a couple of teeth.

All around my neighborhood's misery,
the right combinations hover, dance,
whisper into ears of otherwise
devout members of the Holy Name.

When the pot's really big, Maya gives out
free coffee at Lew's Luncheonette. The Botanica
can't keep the African gods/saints candles in stock.
It's up to 80 mil, somebody says, half whispering.
I don't need that much.

Shit, emits wino Pete,
don't jinx me with that modest shit. I'll take
whatever them motherfuckers give.

No one ever wins. Everyone knows someone
who would have won, if only they had followed
their hearts, or remembered an address, or
been born on a lucky day.

For a while, the block turns lively, almost festive,
then sinks back into its perpetual decay—
cancer, layoffs, ancient rancor that explodes
when the mistress shows at the funeral parlor,
when the strung out junkie steals his mother's rings,
whenever we realize *almost* only counts in horseshoes.

And no one plays horseshoes on my street.

First Grade

Amid Lysol, eraser crumbs, and sweaty hands
Johnny Kazuba was forced to help me with my
penmanship which, according to Sister George, was
seven circles of hell lower than chicken scratch.
Johnny had a tiny nose pinched by enormous
maple syrupcolored glasses. Everyone (the nuns
and cafeteria ladies) said he'd be a priest one day.
Twenty years later, he overdosed on smack but
for all I know, his penmanship was still intact.

"Just a spoonful of sugar helps the medicine go down,
the medicine go down, the medicine go down..."

Julie Andrews, according to Sister, was a saint.
How else to explain that thrilling, bell-pure voice?
My brother, an aficionado of sexual bliss in unlikely places,
claimed Julie had the most spectacular tits in Hollywood.
At six, neither tits nor sainthood wooed me.
I wanted to make perfect Catholic, Palmer-method P's and Q's.

"Edelweiss, edelweiss, every morning you greet me."

I dreamed Julie Andrews spun madly down the rows
where we were seated according to our "God-given IQs,"
displaying her well-bred yet spectacular English tits.
Johhny Kazuba was somber and whispered, "Sorry"
as sister forced him to cup his hand on mine over
the paper I had torn, trying to write like a normal kid.

"Julie Andrews has excellent Palmer Method, children,"
Sister said, "I have her autograph as conclusive evidence."

Johnny's moist, pudgy-child's hand moved, clasped mine
in miserable synchronicity, making one large circle
entwining another—the spiral helix of failure,
two doomed figure skaters carving figure eights

in the ice of an unlined and merciless universe,
while the paper tore, and tore, was rent
like the curtain before the ark of the covenant,
my moron's tears splotched the page.

"I could have danced all night, I could have danced all night!"

And my shame already ancient by age six sang back:
"Fuck you, fuck you, fuck you."

Ethics for Huey O'Donnell

So a friend comes over and you hand him
six big squash, and a nice purple eggplant,
and three or four zucchini from your garden,
the soil still clinging to the fruit of your labors,
your hands still smooth and dirty,
and the friend has something to tell you:

He's got a rare and virulent cancer,
six months maybe to live,
and you put your arms around him because,
hey, that's what friends do,
but you feel nothing at that moment, nothing because
cancer and virulent and six months to live are just words,

and the guy standing before you is tall and handsome,
wearing the same stupid cowboy belt you could never
get away with wearing, and he is going to die.
He doesn't look like someone who is going to die.
He looks like the guy women hurt you with
by saying: "Do you think Huey might…"

He's the guy whose ass your own mother checked out,
and, for all your genuine affection for him,
you have often wished him dead, or a little less blessed
with good looks and now he is going to die. You feel
many official and unofficial things, none of which match,
but your greatest feeling at the moment is anger.

How can you tell me this when I have just given you
a big purple eggplant? This is what you would say,
if you had no editor between your mouth and your heart,
and then you would punch him, and knock his glasses off, and
smash the veggies in his hands, and really hug him—with all
the fear of a true friend, a true friend, but also a false

and the false wins now because that's what he needs—
the one who will say the expected things, who will not

tell him how you envied him all of your life,
and part of you is glad he's the one who is dying, and not you,
and yet you love him with all your lack of integrity—
like a big fucking eggplant still covered with dirt, the stem

quivering like an umbilical—infantile, beyond the decorum
you now uphold, knowing that awkwardness, and platitudes,
and the fine art of "that sucks" is all he or you can handle,
the falsity—the loving falsity Cordelia could not manage.
Oh and how you hate that bitch, Cordelia, who was so virtuous,
she couldn't tell her father a single kiss-ass lie.

There is a maw into which even the best feet dangle,
and we are fed to our deaths and why say the truth
now when you've been avoiding it all these years—
whatever it is, whatever it is, you're not sure,
except you love him, and feel nothing right now
and say: wait a minute...I forgot to give you

some tomatoes, and trudge back out into the warm
late summer light, glad to flee for a moment, and it is only when he
takes one tomato in his hand, having put down the bounty
for a moment, and feels its heft, and juggles it
like a ballplayer waiting for a game, that you cry,
and, when you come to—rise up from the animal self,
you're in his arms, and he's telling you to chill. It's alright.
And it's not alright. And that's alright, too.

I Am What I Remember

The stolid, heavy-lidded gaze
of a giant sea turtle
on whose back I rode when I was five
still troubles me in dreams,

though surrounded in memory
by the repossessed and garish
furniture of my uncle John:
an alcoholic diabetic
who died an hour before the repo-men
could haul away his life.

On his lap lay a plate
of blue and cracked chintz,
and, on his spit-shined Oxfords,
a wedge of tuna sandwich.
For all his desperation he was
natty, clean, precise,
a man who calmly, and with little fuss
assumed his death.

I am only what I remember:
the brief, peripheral touch
of a woman's hand
on my lower back
as she squeezed past me
in the seventh grade,
the scent of chalk dust and henna,
her breasts pressed against my back
still troubling me in sleep,
the hand still sinking in.

And where does it end?
My uncle told me once
I could take my plastic shovel
and dig a hole all the way to China.

He was lying. Memory lies,
but its touch remains

inscrutable and sure
as the sound of an old Victrola
softly hissing behind a voice,
until it becomes half the tune.

The turtle rises slowly,
his long neck strains
forth from the shell, stretches
until the tendons seem
on the verge of snap,
and my father says:
Joseph, smile for chrissakes.
And my mother pleads:
*Come on, sweetie, look up at
the camera,* as I begin to wail.

Somehow knowing this turtle and me
are in deep shit, that this horror,
this crucifixion is no fun day at the zoo.
I am the turtle's cry.

And I hear the tired voice
of the photographer, a three-inch
ash on his stogy, remark:
A bit touchy, ain't he?
And the camera flashes,

that picture lost six houses ago,
a life time repossessed.

How heavy the lids of the turtle,
and of my uncle, and now mine—

with sleep or its absence?
What can you do?

The furniture waits to be lifted,
the props of a life carried off
and to where? I don't know.

Slowly, in the merciless
light of the flash,
the turtle blinks, and,
rising on his limbs, eyes hooded,
begins to crawl.

Poem for Advent

The world takes us at its leisure
slowly, by increments of infamy
or "virtue"

and beyond that taking
we wager freedom
against our corpses,
trick ourselves into living

fully—whatever fully means.
I am writing this in the dust
of an old Chrysler,
its lascivious grill, its chrome
freckled with rust,

it's front end grinning
like Burt Lancaster
in *Elmer Gantry*.

What do I mean?

A million-dollar grin,
the atavistic power of healthy teeth

might convert a nation (see Joel Osteen),
might make us believe in
the power of "abundance."

But suppose I write:

"Lack is the necessity of being."

The nation will turn against me.

The sun is a used car salesman.
To get something for almost nothing
is the pitch of grifters and of angels.
And I have been both
con and evangelist.

"Fear not," says Gabriel.
(The usual line—
see *Britannica*, 1962: how an angel gets one foot in the door.)
"For the Lord of Lords has chosen you."

And the little girl inside us nods her head.

"Yes."

The birds cheep.
Bird twitter and angelic hosts are all around us.

I am postponing the inevitable
until further notice.

Pregnant with God,
I write in the dust of an old Chrysler,
all the sins of the ones with stones.

Slowly they turn away,
and I am left with the woman
taken in adultery,
and I am left with my own
trembling girl, who kneels
in the deepest part of my sarcasm,

beyond all cons, who cries

Maranatha! Who waits
that the spirit might shadow her,
that the womb might not be empty,
that, even in despair, the soul might
feel its worth, and, feeling it,
despair more deeply into joy—this dark thing
that comes to save us from our "truths,"

this dark season where poverty is blessed.

Vesper

At night, when the piano becomes a bird
and glides over the gas company building,
I sink my fingers into keys,
playing the sore back and tired eyes
of my beloved.
And who's to say this music isn't real?
From the edge-lit reeds of rivers,
from the shadows of undercut banks,
one dark, consoling voice
swims out, abandoning its lair.
All over the earth, there's
the long wake of things in passing,
and the ghost of an egret
folding her ancient wings.

Things I Want to Do Before I Die

I want to curl up in a slightly dark and
leathery library—naked—on a cold marble floor
in the fetal position
and remove from her feet slowly, with great reverence,
the spiked high heels of Sophia Loren.
I want to talk intelligently,
and at length,
about olive oil, its history and tradition,
the light on the olive groves at, say, two o'clock,
when siesta is nearly over, and I am awakened
from a nap in the arms of the olive master's daughter.
I want to know how to braid hair.
I want to whistle for a cab. I have never done so,
nor have I lit a match off my shoe, nor have I
stood in a vast wheat field at dusk in Idaho,
squinting towards the horizon, in the full knowledge
that I am the "heart" of America, and may even be
its next president.
I want a statue of me erected right next to Balzac
in the courtyard of MoMA
and I want to see a cardinal light
on my bronze dome as the snow falls and various
high-fashion models sit in rapt silence, admiring my likeness.
In lieu of all this, I would like to look both elegant and eloquent
for just one hour—my shoes shined, shirt tucked,
everything in place, and sing the Agnus Dei perfectly
while one yellow leaf fell from the eighty-foot
ginkgo tree in the Episcopalian
graveyard on Broad Street in Elizabeth
where I used to sit for hours reading
when I was a boy and didn't think of death.

Improvisation on a Theme by Auden

Poetry makes nothing happen
and thank God,
I like the barely swaying
goldenrod
firmly entrenched, its roots in that black soil,
bee-humped, this golden ragamuffin weed
that grows all golden, and has gone to seed.

Listen: Hear the last bee of the year,
deep in the pollened fur, its slender legs
glutted with what makes the bear suspend
five hundred pounds of self to swat the hive,
what would we not do to stay alive
for something sweet?
For something worth
the sting?
She called me names, she called me not at all,
and I rose up and swung my claws. The air
was not impressed. It didn't feel a thing,
the hive was in the mind, not in that tree
against the air, bear like an angry bee
swung deep into its sorrow and its rage,
tore nothing, was paid nothing as its wage.
What good's desire if it doesn't win?
Go ask the bear, he labored, he should know.
The goldenrod nods to what winds might blow
beyond the getting and the almost got,
it keeps a still and unassuming spot
upon my hill, does nothing, rides the breeze,
and, in the fall, makes horny lovers sneeze.

Poet As a Young Voyeur

The little blue house
with its cedar bark shingles,
and the little tree
a miserable sterile pear,
and the little old lady
with the yapping schnauzer,
stopping to berate
her perfectly bald husband,
and the husband swinging
his garden hose violently
in futile protest
as she goes inside—
as if he were mowing down
house tree wife
with a Thompson sub
and all of it seen by the poet
as he sits in the tree house,
eight years old, crew cut,
having grown tired
of the big-breasted cleavage
in the vampire comics

and then Venus rises, evening star
over the billboard of the Marlboro Man,
horse cantering through snowdrifts,
a cigarette dangling
from his tightlipped and determined mouth,
and he looks up at the planet
a bright white-blue
in the gloaming
and notices the bald man
is looking, too,
as if his real life
were there
where a jet climbs
out of Newark airport
into the approaching dark
that swallows them whole.

I Was a Cougar Hunter

The old man in the auto repair shop
where I am busy waiting for a car
that can't be fixed
tells me he was a cougar hunter

out West, he says, he's a Chickasaw.

And he never shakes my hand
or says hello, but begins:

I was cougar hunter.

Why should I doubt it? The creases in his face
are ravines, and the eyes scratch their
blue flint to my face,
until I ignite and become
the small fire that knows his voice:

Yep, hunted 'em in the Dakotas.

He claims there were pretty girls
in Bismarck, big Swedish girls, but they all got fat.

Ain't that the way?

His wife was pretty. Now she's dead.
Good woman. Never gave him a bit of trouble.

There's cougar here, you know,
he tells me, they're coming back.

He can feel out a cat, he says, they're here.

And I believe him. I believe the cougars
are here even now in these hills,
bringing down the deer, waiting out
the groundhogs in their dens.

He goes out to his car
to fetch a walleye lure.
See them teeth marks?
Been a lot of wallys in my life.

When he leaves, my friend asks
why the nut jobs always talk to me.

I am seeing a cougar stalk
through drifts of snow.
I don't know.

Dandelions

Gone to seed gone to
gosling, old lady fuzz,
gone from the bright
yellow,
gone things—ugly stalk
and spores I kick

with my work boot
to watch the seeds
explode—the violence

with which I kick the dandelions,
the tenacious, imperturbable
bane of lawn love.

I love no lawn. I love
these wasted, little hags
I kick.

They are mine. They are mine:
they are the old bitches
at 6 o'clock mass

who always and never die,
someone's grandma I hoist
on the steel toe of my boot.

I kick her to the moon.
She cries: *touch me.*
The things of this world

cry, *touch me.* The things
of this world cry,
dandelion.

Dead Things

That rooster I found on the
tenth floor of the Fairmount Luxury Apartments,
just wandering around in the hall,
Rhode Island Red, fierce,
and coming towards me with his spurs...

How did he get there?

Or the time I was struck in the back of the head
by a pineapple that had somehow
been catapulted from a truck,
and I woke ten minutes later,
with a beautiful Egyptian woman
leaning over me,
her breath smelling miraculously
of coconuts, the intense sadness of her eyes,
not for me, but for every humiliated
and haphazard thing:

What is it?
And how do I know she was Egyptian?

I must have asked her, or perhaps misremembering
is a form of prayer.

What have I not misremembered
so that even your hand, beloved,
resting on mine, now,
and tracing the pale blue vein
just below the knuckle
dissolves into a vast mistake,

a fen of almost-theres
that are never just so
just so this hour of being real—

the cup, the long-ago voices
of family,
the sobs I hear come out from my own throat—

this animal that walks away from inside me,
this thing I have sought to kill,

my spurs slicing the air, my crown
of feathers bristling as I rage,
my life out of place, and not

my life at all.

Dignity

The dog, a yellow Lab
was lying in the street
freshly hit by

a green Oldsmobile
driven by some old lady
who wept

as the crowd gathered
and the kid who owned the dog
ran over

to kneel in the street
to pet him while he
panted, his coat

smeared with blood, his
eyes wild with pain
and yet he licked her face—

the salt of her tears,
and she stroked his head
until the cops showed up

with everyone gathered around
the dying animal
except the old lady

who spoke no English,
who looked like
she might pass out

in a black coat,
her pocketbook
clutched to her chest,

removed from the innocent,
her white hair glowing
red in the siren light.

And I put my arm around
her—the murderer
who smelled of peppermints

and whiskey.

Wanting to Lick the Instep of Your Foot While You Read Larry Levis

I want to lick the instep of your foot
when you put on your reading glasses,
and, sitting primly propped on both feet,
read me a poem by Larry Levis.

There are a thousand desires,
peripheral lusts that, if mentioned,
would ruin my sterling reputation.

Yes. Larry Levis is certainly a great poet.
But what would Larry do?

I imagine Elizabeth Bishop
going down on her South American lover,
the crazy one, who killed herself
in Bishop's Manhattan digs.

Bishop wrote "One Art" about that loss.
It does not mention
the taste of another woman.
Nothing is less memorable or portable
than sex, which is why we keep having it,
hoping it will stick this time—
why it is always new, if we count
not just the act itself, but all the
little acts that make us yearn for
something beyond whatever it is
we are currently pretending to do.
I kiss the hands that hold the book
and you swat me away, wanting me to listen.
I want to listen. I do.
Larry Levis is certainly a great poet.
But what would Larry do?

Elizabeth Bishop found the body
and composed a villanelle.
Disaster and lust must be bound
like Isaac to the rock.
They must be given shape.
The knife poised to strike.
And what God calls time out,
and sends an angel to
withhold the willing hand?

Mercy is a matter of suspension.
Suspended, I will my ears to hear.
This poem is important to you.
It is by Larry Levis.
It makes the hairs stand up
on your slender arms.

But, if one foot comes out
from under your ass, I swear
I will grab it, and hold it in my hands.
Because I like you better than Larry Levis.
That's why I'm listening.
That's why I pretend to hear.

Whatever the Heart Was Given to Chew

I once wanted a life in which my biggest problem
was a cheaper way to caulk the windows:
I wanted a sliding glass door that looked out
on Portuguese tiles, and an aqua pool,
and a friend or two to support
as long as they didn't lean too heavily
upon me.
I wanted a lawn with a well-lit sprinkler system
and, when the occasional bad and young
and pretty girl frolicked in its well-lit splendor,
and wet her halter so that her nipples
stood erect, I wanted a fine and nuanced
discontent, a brief sigh, a sadness like early autumn
to fall on my well-aged, but fully functioning cock.

And I would go into the house and fuck
my middle-aged, but well preserved wife
in a way I hadn't fucked in years,
gripping the bed board till my knuckles
paled, slamming her into bliss.

Normal is as normal does.
The feeble pulse of happiness
is the only pulse I ever wanted to take,

Instead, I was homeless,
and the twitter of birds made me angry
and I lost my heart and my teeth,
and no longer know the difference.

What is a heart?
The yellow light
from other people's houses
takes me in its jaws. Satan has nothing
on the suburbs. Now
I would settle for a different

flavor of sadness—one more bland,
more chewable, easier to spit out
on those who never claimed me.
The grass is bending in the wrong direction.
The wind must feel venial.
A sudden interest in Jesus won't work.
To a man acquainted with suffering,
numbness becomes a balm, and embalmed
he walks carefully over the same terrain
thinking it will somehow be different,
somehow it will be alright if he takes just
the right amount of steps, a sort of spell
he knows all the words to, but cannot
utter—as if the child in him,
the one he has murdered, will rise from the dead,
and everything will be forgiven,
everything—as if the heart could grow teeth
and swallow whatever it was given to chew.

Filthy River

I live near a filthy river.
I have always lived near a filthy river,
and yet the nymphs climb the metal netting
of half-submerged shopping carts to sing to me!

What do they sing? Sometimes it's Palestrina,
and sometimes its Marvin Gaye.
Often I tie myself to the mast of a ship,
so as to be seduced but not
led away
into death. Occasionally,
I listen and drown.

I drown in a filthy river.
I have always drowned in a filthy river
to rise like Osiris with the dawn,
to sink in the mud that I know
is the source of all song.

I would ask you to join me,
but you swat your arms
and complain about the mosquitoes.

Let them bite, draw blood.
You will remember a song
from your childhood
or the first good kiss, or the way
light played on your legs the first time
you knew they were pretty.
Don't be afraid. I have made this poem
for you to enter. Enter the river.
The mud between your toes
is your mother. The sun on your freckled back
knows your name.
Willow thy hair, and roots thy limbs.
Climb the netting of half-submerged shopping carts.
Sing Palestrina or Marvin Gaye. Sing in the river
until only the song remains.

New and Uncollected Poems (2006–2013)

Quote: Four Potatoes

"I remember boiling four 'new' potatoes (those are the small ones others call salt potatoes) making myself a small saucepan of melted butter with pepper, and eating the potatoes whole and skewered on my Swiss army blade as I read Williams's *Selected Poems.* I was 18 years old, and the only one awake in the house at three in the morning. It is one of the happiest memories of my life. Maybe it was the linoleum which was torn just under my seat. I scratched an itch on my bare foot with it. Maybe it was the florescent light. It could have been Williams's poems, too, but I know, know beyond all doubt that, without those four potatoes, no happiness would have been as possible."

The Plumber's Apprentice

I can't forgive myself for being a "poet."
Plumbers make more money
and, unlike me, they are useful.

I look down at my chubby hands and say:
Aren't you tired of metaphors?
Don't you want to grip a lug wrench?

I want to stop using the things my
mother said the world had too much of:
WORDS,
more ways of saying: light, tree, waterfall,
wolf, penguin, egret, knee sock, lick.

I envy the plumbers, the way they know
what sings and prays, what burbles within our walls,
the way they say: elbow joint, sprocket, arc weld, knurl—

Hey, who am I kidding? I envy their words,
the certainty with which they pluck them forth,
to sing the song of pipes, and valves, to make the
secret vital world that we ignore.

Let me build then in the house of my poems,
the right flow of lines,
nothing clogged—a labyrinth
of
gleaming copper, brass,
every joint and seamless weld
a press fit—snug, so that the shit might flow
more readily, and all my sewers be blest.

The Pear Tree in My Yard

Always loved the word yard,
always loved that ugly thing
it did to my mouth,
voiced without teeth or hardly any breath,
this sound as homely as my life.

It is not like Lolita tapping at the teeth
at three, it is the
absence of making busy with a tongue.
And now the pears are falling
bottom-heavy from their stems,

breaking, and again unbroken
in the dark uncut grass
where deer come nuzzle them,
frost quickens their brandy ooze
fallen for whatever ants might pray

for windfalls. Sweet Christ, what grace
has brought me down to you?
This gravity so fierce it forces me to rise.
 And through midnight I can
hear stems break, the softest thud—

the round pears drop, the death of me
is blest. I want to die, that something
can be fed, beyond the lie I am
the quiet death of me, pull me down oh Lord
in the night wind where the white flowers

blew all frazzled. How many months before?
A thousand years it seems.
When spring raged through night orchards,
in the first warm rains, before the leaves
were born. This, too, is birth. This

too—to drop and be deer nuzzle,
to be death. Come, ripe, maturing sun.
Thy will be done.

A Dream of Elephants

Suppose someone kissed my ears tenderly,
ignoring those lynx-like tufts of hair
peculiar to men who have to work hard
at being loved,
and she said: Awww...my little Savannah dust,

would I smile?

The years go by. That's what years do.
They go by, and the tusks grow long,
and my ears remain unmolested.

I am lonely in supermarkets.
Once, when I was young...
(it's enough to say that to make a room grow empty).

Once, when I was young,
I dreamed I was a man with
a pimple in the middle of my forehead
the size of Greece,

and I was in a vast Catholic school gym
cleaning up after Saturday night bingo,
and all the old people lay there dead,
as if a sniper had entered the room
and shot them cleanly through the head.

Tenderly, I placed bingo chips
on all their eyes to pay their boat fare over Lethe
or was it the river Jordan? Anyway,
I knelt reverently over each—

the fat lady with the pillbox hat,
the old and gentle closet queen
who had never married and who danced
the cha-cha with all the other men's wives.

It was so peaceful there.
I wanted to lay down
and place chips over my own eyes
and wait for Gabriel's horn to blow
but God said: "No!"

and when I rose, I saw the elephants!

There were hundreds, gamboling about,
swirling dust, defecating on the corpses
of third-degree knights,
doing what elephants supposedly do.

I was not afraid.
At a certain point in life,
anything can happen to you and it does.

They sang to me telepathically:

"Lay down your weary head. Lay down."

It was an old hymn. It was beautiful.
After a certain point, you don't care anymore,
and the cheap songs seem no longer cheap,
and you start to believe them all.

My old ninth grade English teacher showed up.
"Joseph, why so many ands?"

I explained I was in love with the conjunctive,
with the bridge between the living
and the dead.
"You will have it hard," she said
and disappeared.

I woke then with a stiff neck, a stiff conscience,
a stiff dick. I was stiff, an old man
clutching at his dreams.
I have always been old.
I have always stared at lawns, or lakes, or women
as though they were waving goodbye.

What does not wave goodbye?
Who does not stand at the shore of grief
raising a cherished arm?

I cherish all thy arms.
I call you thou.
I wait for the voice to whisper:
"My little savannah dust."

I am drinking too much amaretto.
It must wax as the coffee wanes.
It is Sunday and I am drunk.
The hour has come
and will keep on coming. The years go by.
That's what years do. They go by,
and who would I not shoot
for tenderness?
And who would I not exalt
in the shadows of my body?

In the middle of an elephant's skull
I have placed a ruby.
The field I have bought
at a great price is overgrown.
I like the weeds. I have forgotten the pearl!

Chicory, sweet Timothy, Queen Anne's lace,
efface the greed in me. The pearl is this poverty
towards which I rise—this naught I am.

This is my heaven.
Bring forth the herd!
Have them trumpet my arrival.

I have come to bless the weeds
to sing the wound. It is fresh. And it never heals.
I have come among the elephants
to raise the shadow of a tree, to fix it
strong against the sky.
Then, tenderly, my eyes will let it go.

My Mother Reading in the Land of the Dead

There were ghosts who had come to touch her, hear her musings
as she lay there reading aloud from the broken trees.
There were those who had come to hear her mispronounce

the names of God, each misplaced syllable another wound
through which they could have entered, could have tramped
barefoot back into life and been risen and at ease.

They would have laughed to nudge the snow-wet roots of birches,
cried out to feel the cold rush against their skins, the sharp,
quick pinch of thorns, the jay's fierce cry, cried out in joy

when their blood welled and ran, and listened as she lay there
reading from out of the broken trees, pierced by the thousand voices
the names of God, each misplaced syllable another life

which in those ears, and in those spent and silent fields
took on the shape of being, the blue ferocity
of a jay, and spoke for her the life that she had lost.

When I am No Longer Human

for Miguel Hernández

When I am no longer human, then I will be human,
when I am no longer visible except as sound,
a low groan in the mind of a passerby,
then I will be neither night nor day,
but dusk as I was meant to be.

A place in the vast sky that is no place.
A hunger that belches as if it were a feast—
contradiction at peace with death, with life,
at war with contradiction.

Come to me, you who were so beautiful,
and whom I desired and was too cowardly
to fully take—
come and pass through me, ghost of my living.

Failure, sit at my feet, I can finally write you.
I can place my hands upon your head,
and give you blessing.

Die into me, all that I wanted, all that I gathered up.
My hands are open to release you.
You break your wings against me,
against the first star and the last.

Pratfall

In a dark time, or something to that effect—
let's say, in the midst of having no midst
with which I am happy,

I purposely fall down the stairs.
It is something to do—
a tumble that may or may not injure,
a way to break through the conventional
sadness, and have a real problem:

broken ribs, fractured skull, something
to take my mind off my sorrows.

I want a new palette of woes!
The canvas on which I paint my misery
is too thick, too impasto.

A kiss from an unlikely stranger
or even a likely one might be
a sort of turpentine—something
to wash away the blues, the mean reds.

Where is ocher when you really need it?
And sienna brown?

The brushes are stiff. I want to spin
out of this sense of doom—

false friends, false cheer, false teeth!
Could I not be an old man in a nursing home
pinching a nurse on the ass with his dentures?
Or a species of rare mushroom?
Or a kite—
torn in the telephone wires, tattered,
the "keys to my success"
causing the volts to surge until

my body has no sense of the mind
that disdains it? Oh I am sick—the rank smell
of me on my own sheets. My hands
have become unwanted guests.
I would send them towards a piano
or a pretty neck, but they refuse
to do anything but type.

And now I must teach, and what?
The clown knows how to fall.
The stairs are waiting.
Lean into the weather of grief
and drop.

Summer School 1974

Elizabeth River runs pink
on hot summer days
from Pearl Street down to
Morris Avenue—

a pink river!

And I'm in summer school
for failing math and Spanish.

I like to fail.
Something in me wants
to tear off all the scabs:
bleed more, bleed more

until this anger's pink.

Whoever painted the river
is, no doubt, a success.

The world is full of money
and angry failures
and pink rivers.

The girl who is a Jesus freak
and hangs in the Jesus bookstore
has a nice ass.

Lesser things have led to
my conversion.

We kiss—two failures,
one angry, and one saved.

She has Jesus.
I have a hard on.

All through Spanish
in this sweltering room
where all the failures go

I stare at her copper-colored hair.

She is surprised I know
the Sermon on the Mount.
She is shocked when I
quote Paul.

I tell her
the river will catch fire
if I light a match to it.

The men who did this
love God, but not rivers.

My mother has cancer.
If I could, I would shoot
everyone except this girl.

I would like her mouth
to save me. Jesus
has no tongue, no breasts.

I stared at him for fifteen hours
once, begging him
to come down from his cross.

It was after they drew the grid
on my mother's skull.
It was after her breath
almost made me puke.

Jesus saves
men who make rivers run pink.

My mother begs me
not to be so angry.
I tell the girl
fuck Jesus. This only makes me

a challenge. She says:
she'll pray for my mother.
I tell her thanks and feel her breasts.
She lets me.

When she visits my house
it stinks of cancer. My mother
wears her hooded bathrobe.
The girl is scared.

After that, she doesn't want to kiss.

The face of Christ takes
all the fun out of being saved.
It's bad for making out.

I don't blame her.
I don't blame anyone.
My mother is crying.
I tell her to drink her tea.
I tell her everything will work out.
I tell her the prayers will work.
I know I am full of shit.

While the World Is Falling Apart, I Open a Jar of Pickles

Salvation is vulgar, so, too, destruction
calling for poems we know won't last
into the next stasis, the next ho hum.

Some have accused me of liking drama.
But I am standing here, opening a jar of pickles,
the pleasing sound of a vacuum relenting,
poof! And then the kosher dill, the baby
sweet gherkin, the fragrant scent of pickling
spices wafting over me. Voila!

I am in a kitchen late at night,
opening a jar against all evils, the
stupid deaths, and illnesses, and failures—
a little boy in the near dark, bare foot
against the scarred linoleum, my heart the only true justice,
pounding—fuck it all, fuck it all.
If you slice these thin enough
the veil becomes translucent, and the dead return.
They sit down at table, steam of their tea
rising. I know. It's late, and my feet make no din.
I have risen. How many times? It's a cheap trick!
Blessed the jar, blessed the left hand twisting,
blessed the unspectacular effort—a sandwich.
Sliced thin, the pickles will not overwhelm
the smoked turkey, and the provolone.
At three in the morning, when everything is merciless,
when my heart is the only justice. It is strong.
It will do its job. It will knock and knock
until the door is opened.

Love Poem for My Mother, Clare

Why should a chipmunk bring you back,
or the solemn throb of lightning without the thunder's sound,
or, treading on thin ice, that odd familiar crack
I loved as a child and risked my life to hear?

Come to me now, if only as some pain
my stealthy soul keeps longing to decode,
to see your son—bald, unsettled, vain,
a man who trips on pants cuffs, laces, love

and shake your finger or hide your face for shame,
but come—rise from the pantry's onion skins,
and only speak the fullness of my name,
then who would care for losses, or for wins?

There's not a loss or win enough to raise
you from the dead. Forgive my greed.
I should be satisfied to stumble on
and find you at odd hours: stone or weed,

snow-covered, random, in some sudden thing
that, for no reason, brings my grieving back
as sharp as when you died, that brings you here
where I'm as old as you were when you left.

Star light, star bright, whatever may suffice.
Look Mah! I'm dancing! And the world is ice.

From the Book of Mistranslations

Who am I to be so mistranslated into being?
And who comes to make all the necessary corrections?

The peonies looked like they were brooding this spring,
and the lilacs, well, I felt insane
for admiring their leaves more than their flowers.

Things break. The hand of a lover
can sweep grandly over the landscape,
sweep the parked Volkswagon and the
far-off mountains away.
And what of it?
There is a certain romance to erasure,
the way her hand moved as I lay
sprawled on the flood wall's grass,
plucking a dandelion with my toes.

We are not here, even when we are.
This is not sad. The last light, and the
first gold finch, and the way her mouth
moved over mine—all this verbiage and
foliage, and the dark shade under the lilacs—
the smell of dirt.

This must be what I mean:
leaves, and shade, and the bright red
Volks, its lights clicking on as she leaves,
and for a long time,
for a long time,
for a long time,
I can feel her hand on my knee.

Kiss

It's been a long time.
The sky above the Gulf station sign
is cerulean, and orange like the sign,
and there is a dog barking in the kingdom of dogs,
and the wind is causing the flag pole to flog itself.

No hour ever loved itself more than this:
kiss, and the blood makes sense—
the way our lips swell, the way I
can't seem to stop, the violence
of holding you, how I have crushed myself
against you, as if to make a likeness,
something that will last, that won't last,
that—
I stand back, just a little to note
the way orange and cerulean have
gathered at your throat, the wind, and
the dog baying now, and the
flag pole's relentless ping!

It's all there. In your eyes,
telephone wires, and the clouds heading
northward, being torn along the highway.

Paying, we buckle up: Tic Tacs, Vitamin Water,
the way I reach for the shift, and your hand
over mine. Why can't I disappear with you,
right now before everything goes wrong?
The flag pole is telling the truth.
The violence of love makes me sad.
Your hand is dry and warm, and squeezes mine.

This will fade. I am too intense to
let love sit down. I scare myself.
I have always scared myself.
"You'd rather have poems than me."

The voice of an old love is like that flogging pole.
It beats itself in the wind. It's not true, it's not true.
It is. Your hand rubs my shoulder.
We are going somewhere. You bring both knees up,
so agile, sit with your toes clenching
the lip of the passenger seat. You take my free hand
in yours and kiss it, place it to your cheek.
I am so scared, so scared I am only words. So scared.
You let my hand fall to your lap.
The first star has risen. Relax.

For Chávez

Chávez is dead. Because of this, there
are rivers running backwards in the world
and this poem is full of passive verbs.

Chávez, there will be no outwitting
the rich who only lose to death,
and not even then. Their tombs

are major gold exhibitions, their eyes
reach all around the poor. They
encircle the fat diamond

which the pressure of thousands
of workers has made—coal
crushed to whiteness, hard and beautiful

and without mercy. It is your mercy
that does not die—even if it only hobbles.
In dreams, I see it floating like ashes

above the carnival. I see it
in the vapor of a man's breath—
his cracked skin intimate with the cold.

I believe in mercy, Chávez. I am
one of the stupid ones who
will continuing carting your heart

through the streets in my wheelbarrow.
It is covered in shit. How else
will a heart survive? Like everything

true, it will stink, and the better people
will disown it. Chávez, I am tapping
gently on your poor boy's skull.

I am crying because God still
makes idiots—holy or otherwise.
Because the work is far

from done. Because you
were not an idiot, because I
am prone to weeping. Forgive me.

My hand is reaching into the dark
and pulling out a heart
beating wildly in space.

Lark of my house—a bird's heart
fierce and alien, and alive, though no one
may see it—as tiny as it is.

It pounds in the moonlight the poor
are forced to eat and which
they devour—hour into hour.

Poor boy, Chávez, *El Presidente,*
rest beneath your minions:
this pickax, this shovel, this cry.

On Reading Keats at Age Fifteen

You knew when the sky turned a Coke bottle green,
when the rain poured down and named your street
in its own peculiar syllables.
You knew that there was something wrong
because you were fifteen and reading
Keats's "Ode to a Nightingale" and loving it.

You came to the part where Keats wrote:
"Darkling, I listen, and for a long time, now,
I have been half in love with easeful death."
You read those words until you wore them smooth,
until thunder scored the trees and scared the dog
who had been keeping time, flogging the rug
with his tail.

Outside the trees rose and swayed,
mad figures in a Martha Graham work.
What was your dissatisfaction, your disdain,
for everything and everyone?
Your longing had no aim except to long.
To what could you have attached
these figures in your dance?

Everything was sad—cast out,
the furniture, summer, Keats,
who knew a drowsy numbness, knew
his lack was some necessity of being,
some vast essential sleep from which
only a word or a girl might have waked him.
You had no words, no girl, no silver veins to kiss,
imagining the veins in girl's slight wrists
smelled of rain and deep, delved earth.

Something was growing in you, something
beyond Keats, beyond the word forlorn,
and, darkling, you kicked the book away

and stood, for a long time, looking out the window,
tracing a drop of rain
with your finger down the glass.

Googling the Clam

I Google search the clam.
My wife, being of a gentle disposition,
not wanting to eat what thinks or feels,
makes mind and heart condition for devouring.

It must not have a mind, it must not have a heart.
It must not dream of a past life in Brooklyn;
it must not have
residual memories
of playing the violin
or kissing wounded soldiers.

It must push itself along the sea bottom
with a singular "foot"—that part
I am informed—which tastes a little
"chewy."

She waits. A brain? No darling.
A heart? Something of that sort.
All summer she dipped heart and foot
in melted butter, kissed me with
the kisses of her mouth, swallowed clams
and oysters by the dozen, called me lover
and did not despair.

Compassion now disowns her past transgressions.
I think of the clam beginning life as male
then undergoing a "sea change,"
its sixty million eggs, its progeny spread forth,
a silky luminescence upon the curl of waves.

The clam and the clam and the sea?
The Holy Spirit between the two: the male,
the female, the one, the many, the soft curl
of her hair against my shaven cheek.

They say a transplanted liver can hold
a residual love of Bach. All parts of us
sound forth the heart and mind.

We are devoured, and in the petals of flowers
the memory of sunlight, the symmetry of the spiraled
Nautilus, the clam extending its chewy foot—
the root of love, what goes down
with or without the melted butter,
so that even my cartilage loves her.

Nine Diner Poems

Remembrance

for Terry

Many years ago, a friend wrote: "come to me, softly transcending all the lightbulbs." I thought it was a beautiful line. Sometimes, in the middle of barley soup, I lift my spoon and remember her; my hand shakes because she is dead. I want to come to her, but I'm no good at transcending lightbulbs. Bending over to tie my shoes, I run out of breath.

Favorite Waitress

Where is my favorite waitress? The one with the fading grease burn on her arm shaped just like the island of Sumatra? Has she been carried away by a prince or a lawyer, or a regular customer who plays a mean cello? Suppose she is dressed all in white now, in a gown, like someone who has died and gone to live forever on the Christian Home Network. She is in the choir of the saved. Her regular, the cellist, plays Bach, and Elgar, and choice selections of Bulgarian folk music. Her former pencil and pad dance around her, as they might do in a Disney movie, singing. Is my favorite waitress trapped on the Christian Home Network? In a Disney movie? This is the other side of America. This is the side that seeps into our souls while the parents divorce, and the children wake up from their childhoods addicted to menthol and to texting. It is The Little Mermaid DVD. My favorite waitress would rather be in hell. She would rather be in that place where the rain brings out the smell of the early bird special in her hair, and makes it frizzy, knotted, hard to brush. On her right arm, just above the elbow, lies the island of Sumatra. All the animals are endangered.

The forests are being ravaged. You can see it in her eyes. I have been coming to this diner for ten years, and for ten years I have always sat in her section—if possible. Not once have I smiled, except shyly, imperceptibly. Not once have I kidded her. And she has not smiled, or kidded me. We have an agreement. The tip is always 25 percent. We have created a nation that is not about smiles and kidding. It is a deeply serious kingdom in which sorrow has a place, and no one escapes it. It is a kingdom in which the children fall asleep and wake up addicted to menthol and to texting. I have not seen my waitress now in three weeks. If I ask about her they will say: "She quit." They will say: "Elvis has left the building." They will say, "She died." If I don't ask, then she has been carried away by the good looking health food manager who knows how to surf, who knows what to do with a favorite waitress. He has taken her on a long bus ride to some distant beach town where the waves and the people are always beautiful and high. He kisses the island of Sumatra which lies just above the elbow of her right arm. Perhaps all will be well. Perhaps the animals and the forests will return. They will all start singing. I have been alive long enough to know that few things in this life return, and fewer still are liable to sing, but she is my favorite. She always got the order right. God's speed to her. I suppose, in the end, like most Americans, I am a positive thinker.

What I Knew

When she put an onion ring on her tongue and poked it out at me, I knew we would never be lovers. That's the sort of brazen thing you do after a year of being in love. She was flirting with the moment, not with me. I was her friend. It was late, and the waitress kept tapping her foot, waiting

180

for us to leave. I paid. We left. Before getting into her car she kissed my cheek and told me it was fun. Good night. I watched her pull away, leaving me to adjust the night just a little more closely around my shoulders. Only then did I take my right hand out of my pocket and stare at it—at all the misery that was there on the palm underneath the life line which looked pretty much as it had always looked— only a little more broken and considerably shorter.

Mercy

I love all the food for people with bad teeth: meat loaf, eggs over easy, matzo ball soup. There is something merciful about soft cuisine. They have almost ruined mercy by calling it comfort food. Nothing comforts me—the mashed potatoes, the jaws of an old man chewing, chewing, the harsh light of the diner bouncing off his eyeglasses: he is wearing a plaid shirt. I want to kiss his forehead and watch him rise into heaven. I want him to go away.

Right Now

Right now I am the diner poet. I look at the cake selection (all those wonders of sugar and fluff presented under glass!) but never order any cake. The menus are heavy, heavier than the groaning board, heavier than tribulation. There are always two or three elderly people who eat the liver often enough so that it can never be removed from the menu. I order the liver. I only eat the onions and the bacon…(I want to help their cause).

Ars Poetica

To be all by yourself in a diner, to stare into the coffee
cup and watch the milk disperse, to hear your own spoon
scraping the bottom of the cup...Poetry is nowhere near
as beautiful as the sound of that spoon. That's why I keep
writing it—ambition.

Chicken Fat

In that particular place, at that particular time, there was
a decanter of chicken fat on every table—liquefied, look-
ing not much different than olive oil. You'd put some on
your rye, with a glass of tea. The tea was very beautiful
seen through a glass. On late autumn days, when I am sad
beyond all other hope, I close my eyes and imagine the
tea—amber in the November light, I imagine how the sun
shone on the little park across the street and who sat there
throwing stale bread to a thousand pigeons. It was a place
where a man could take his dentures out—if they were
hurting. I think of all the black coats, and how the snow fell
into them—how it disappeared as quickly as it had kissed
the collars of the men and women who clutched their necks
against the cold. To sit at the table nearest the door was to
experience drafts. The waiter told jokes that weren't funny
unless you laughed at them. His eyes said please laugh. I
would go there to laugh very loudly and eat four slices of
rye with schmaltz. Who isn't a liar in this world. God will
count many things against us, but he will not count the
lies of mercy we tell. Did I tell enough? Dear creator, do
not hold my sins against me. I would like to take out my
dentures but that is not necessary. They were stolen at the
shelter. One size fits all? Halloween? Who knows. But it's
alright. Who needs teeth? I don't plan to date anyone any
time soon. If I laugh you will see the maw into which the

wind is crooning. I forgot the place no longer exists and I walked all the way here. Who am I speaking to? If I could remember one joke the waiter told then perhaps the world would not seem so bad. It does not seem so bad! Look! The blue sky is a heckler! We are all together waiting for the next comedian. A little chicken fat on a slice of rye goes a long way. Don't knock it until you try it.

What It Is to Serve

The young people are enclosed in death, but they don't know it. They laugh and order cheap stuff, and take forever. They leave the waitress hardly any tip. It is good that we send them off to war to learn what it is to serve, but we don't send them off to war, do we? No. Not these children. They are our kids. They have our faces. They wear our arrogance. We send the bus boys instead who tip well, and who serve and who serve until someone's contempt breaks the dishes, and they die.

Closed

A shore town in winter—a closed diner, its parking lot full of trash, and next to its entrance, a dead seagull…this cheers me up. There is something lively about ruins, almost festive. I look at the bird. The bird looks at me. The wind bristles its feathers—slate grey, buff white. I want that two-beat phrase: pull out. It is almost dark, and I can smell the sea.

The Real Killing

Oochie Speaks

I knew this guy used to like killing ants with a magnifying glass. He was nuts for it. He'd catch the sun just right and burn the things up—just toast the little motherfuckers, but he wouldn't step on an ant. No...He'd step on his mother's face and grind her glasses into her eyeballs before he'd step on an ant. That's the point, bro—wherever people got some science to what they do—that's where the real killing is.

Obstructing Justice

In the factory the INS would come
wearing their brand name: INS
and catch the illegals
who were in the act
of almost making a living.

Fat José fell from the forklift basket
some twenty feet and broke his legs,
lay writhing on the oilsoaked floor,

and I thought how they had
broken the legs of the thieves,
but left Christ's bones intact
because he was already dead,

and I thought how I would like to
kill everyone in a suit, and all
Christian Republicans,
and the elitist leftists
in the academy who prattle on
about globalization
and make me ashamed
of ever having read a book,
and the bored students I saw
sipping espressos
in Hoboken cafes,
who had no idea,
and wouldn't have cared
how deadly their boredom is,

but there were not enough
bullets for my rage.
And so I killed no one,
but knelt beside Fat José
who was out of his mind
with pain, drooling, the bone of

his left leg jutting out
from his work pants, his wallet
containing a picture of his daughter
in a communion dress, three singles
and a false ID—
this pudgy father, this "criminal."

And, being the first aid attendant,
and the shop steward,
and the idiot in residence,
I refused to let them cuff him,
and told the INS to go fuck themselves,
stared at the bright letters
on their chests, these clowns of law.
And nothing ever felt more right
when they threatened to arrest me for
"obstructing justice."
It was better than the sweetest sex,
and I was still saying fuck you, fuck you,
when the foreman dragged me away.

The Ooh Ooh People

When I was unemployed due to economic layoff from my factory, I worked for a while as a furniture mover (under the table, twelve bucks an hour and whatever tips you might get). I was over forty by then and I was the box man—a job for younger men with the legs of center fielders. The box man carries all the boxes up and down the flights of stairs. It might seem the easier job compared to moving the heavy furniture, but you go up and down those stairs about a hundred fifty times with sometimes forty pound boxes, and your legs start to feel like they might stage a walk out and let you fall. To your death.

One job we started at six in the morning and finished up at midnight. It was in a rich neighborhood and had an "ooh, ooh" couple. Ooh ooh couples watch you. They stand behind you saying: "Ooh Ooh! Be careful" all the way up the stairs. They can cause accidents just by being under foot every inch of the way. They think you are a Morlock. They usually have children or pets, and if you smile at the children and the pets, they hug them tightly to their chests, and grow wide-eyed, as if you are about to molest them. They believe all working people are trailer trash and thieves and that we love nothing better than to break their precious things whenever we aren't having unprotected sex with our sisters. If you break anything (and they pack terribly) your boss will be sued and you'll get fired. If you want to know who is what in America, work on a moving van.

So this house had a basement the size of a football field. It took sixteen hours at the end of which they made no attempt to tip us. Me and my friend were so tired and sore we went to eat in the only joint left open—this little Mexican place—and fell asleep at the table. The waitress had to wake us up. I worked as a box man for two months until I just couldn't stand it. The work was hard, but the people were harder. They had all stepped out of reruns of *Thirtysomething*

187

and I remember one couple had a beautiful baby grand. Neither could play it. I couldn't help myself. At lunch break I approached them. They had seemed nice enough until then. I said: "That's a gorgeous Bechstein you've got there…could I just play it a little?" They looked at each other like aliens conferring and said in unison: "No." I continued: "Can I hear you play? I love piano." The man said: "We don't play piano. A few of our friends do." I could tell this bit of familiarity had gone too far. I shut up, finished my lunch, and returned to moving boxes.

The piano haunts me. I keep thinking that no piano should lay dormant—a mere display of wealth. I think of all the un-played pianos on this earth, some used as glorified tables for mail, coats, family photos, others kept polished but without a single hand touching their keys. I keep dreaming of sneaking back into that house in the middle of the night and playing the Bechstein. I see the young, attractive couple come down the stairs and they are chastened. "You play well…" They say, "Come stay with us and teach us the ways of your tribe."

It is hard to move pianos you know will seldom be played, harder still to be pursued by Ooh ooh couples as you struggle up the stairs. If you have any spirit left, it makes you angry. What can you do with such anger? You can wait until it turns into sadness, a sadness so deep you can dive into it and never reach bottom, even, though, to all the ooh ooh's out there, you have been at the bottom all your life.

When I Need Quiet

When I need quiet, the whole world wants to blab.
Hardy men in hard hats harrumph their
bold machines: their arms and bicuspids quaking
as they prod the road with bucktoothed jackhammers.

A question flutters in, an ugly moth, to sting my solitude,
a cell phone purrs "Für Elise" or blasts "La Marseillaise,"
and I'm not French, and neither is that hipster girl
who won't answer her phone, and is droning on
about a certain pair of shoes she didn't buy.

They say there is a place in Indiana so silent
that men go mad for want of sound:
a soundproof room the scientists have made.
After an hour the din of your own heart beating
becomes unbearable; an hour later, and you can hear
your own dead pleading with you to join them.
They call it auditory hallucinations, but I wonder....

When I want quiet, it is the dead I always hear
speaking in their tongues of longing
and it is impossible for me to say
anything I mean, and then
they are drowned out by the cars, and I'm alone
again, among the living, cursing the jackhammers.

But sometimes, as the sun goes down
and I want quiet, I actually get it:
and then, one by one, my dead rise to touch my shoulder
softly, lovingly, their hands pressed into the wound
I carry from one noise to the next,
drowned out though they are by what I call a life,
I know that they are there, a pale half-moon
rising in the middle of a sunlit sky—
to give me courage, to keep me
more than sane.

About Light

I was no more than three, bundled up
so that my arms could barely move,
snow frozen to my mittens,
boots already half-filled with snow,
everything wet for the radiator
to spit and spatter dry.

My mother was coming home,
her life full of children
and the stink of drying wool.

Hey mom! Hey mom! I shouted,
my hat lost, ears red,
my unbuckled boots half-way falling off,
the snot of my nose turned to ice.
Hey mom!

And she took my hand, there
where the bus had left her off,
and walked with me,
and I asked:
why are the traffic lights more red when it snows?

And she looked at me a long while,
tears massing at the borders of her eyes,
and said: "You notice such strange things."
And that night, read me "Where Go the Boats,"
and when she came to the part where
the poet wrote: "other little children
shall bring my boat ashore,"
she cried and told me: "keep yourself a secret.
People will spit on you."

And then we stood on the porch
pondering the Christmas lights
strung from all the porches of our neighborhood,
haloed by the cold, bulbs chipped from years of use,
and she said: "You're too forgetful Joseph…
remember your hat, and forget
the red traffic lights in the snow.
"You're just like me…I want you to be happy."

What Heals

What heals?
A long hot bath
in which
I happily lie in my own filth,
leeching color from
already well-leeched flesh,
and stare up winking at the Virgin
who calmly stomps the serpent's skull:

this heals;

or a whole day when I haunt
the rooms of my own house,
hearing the sound of my
wife's bedroom slippers
scratching like a well-sharpened pencil
against the sketch pad of the afternoon.

What heals
is not the closing of wounds,
but their full ripe opening
until I am a river in free flow.

"As rivers we were permanent" I wrote
when I was seventeen,
a poem I never finished.
I've waited over thirty years
to find out if the line is true.

I still don't know.

The bath water chills.
Naked, I scratch my ass,
disdain to use a towel.
Upstairs, YouTube offers
Dinu Lipatti

playing Chopin's
D-flat major Nocturne.

The soft hiss of the ancient record
adds to its glory.
I have left wet footprints everywhere.
I have grown used to my sadness.
We take vacations, pose for photos,
her arm draped over me.
I have made peace with grief.

Dinu Lipatti died
when he was thirty-two.
My mother had just turned fifty.

There is a river where joy and grief
refuse to give their names.
You must guess which is which
and the wrong guess is always right.

These identical twins play tricks,
so in the middle of weeping, I laugh,
and, in the middle of laughing, I weep.
And this house
two hundred miles and fifty years
removed from where I was born
is washed in the same waters,
and is all the houses
in which I have ever lived,
and from which
I am forever exiled.

And It Begins to Rain

Things get torn and light rips through them, is of them, is light, is song, is a bunch of trees at night—the cherry blossoms are like Richard Burton and Liz Taylor at the height of their fame—snapshot beyond all reason. One blossom held to the lip of a beloved—long dead—this sort of thing can "grow" on you. Soon you are Central Park after sunset, a very good eye with some lenses making sure the world stays intact. This is how the world stays intact: we say: "Ah, how cool! Look at the cherry blossoms—anciently sudden and suddenly ancient." Or maybe we don't say anything at all. Maybe we just wear a light spring jacket, and it begins to rain.

A Kind of Suite

1.

The days all slightly flat and out of key.
One could call it a style
until, by chance,
the right note rings.

2.

Goats eat
whatever is available.
People are picky
to the point of starvation
(and to prove they aren't goats).

3.

As a child I watched
the clouds eat the moon
and never grew bored.
This was the beginning of my troubles:
sadness became pleasurable.
Solitude grew enormous, a flower
others called a weed.
I watered it daily.
I learned everything was eating and being eaten.
Swallow yourself. Quick!
The clouds spoke to me
and the moon willingly gave itself.
When I grew older I forgot the principle
of swallowing and being swallowed.
My whole life was a mis-education,
but I have returned
to some vast stupidity.
And now am ready to begin.

4.

The young poet wants to be poetic.
He carves elaborate temples out of ham bones.
He beats us over the head with his genius, and is snide
and arrogant, and the enemy of falsehood.
He wins awards, gets fat around the middle
or stays slender out of vanity. Years later
if he is lucky, the trees stop obeying his metaphors.
He is troubled, or honored beyond his desire for honors.
He grows cranky and wants people to be simple,
like the best fish dishes. He holds court
and is kind and cruel by turns so that
the audience begins reading him—like a poem,
reading his every pause, his every gesture.
If this does not happen, it is worse and he grows bitter
like certain herbs that have been left unpicked- and go to seed.
One night he dreams he is a Ferris wheel.
Everyone on the Ferris wheel is sick and gripping the bars too tightly.
He is tired of poems. They all evaded, or betrayed, or failed him
one way or another. He stops writing poems. What he writes
has lines, and rhythms, and fewer tricks—they are a doodling,
a doodling very much like poetry. He laughs to himself, no longer
cares if others get the joke. He reads his early poems. They are not bad.
They are arrogant and poetic, and are showing off. If they could meet
his later works, they'd probably not be friends. He wants to tell
the younger poet: be simple, like the best fish dishes...
but what is simple? If you try to say what it is, it will
flee from the room. Shut up old man. Scribble a few words.
Say it is a little butter and a dash of wine,
a couple of bay leaves perhaps, all served on a pale, blue plate.
He hates the whores of simplicity.
He doesn't trust the decorative.
Where was it he had that perfect cod, and why do only painters
get to play with the leftover bones?

Glass of Water

My wife is calm, even in the midst of Armageddon,
As for me, I never met a form of hysteria I didn't like.

The world is always falling apart. I took nine different
Homeless people in over three years, four of which
Were from Westchester, and were only temporarily broke
On their way to six figure incomes, and a European tour.

I feel sorry for the rich as well as the poor.
My father told me to pray for the rich.
They starve their kids, he said.
And those poor little bastards never get second helpings.

Why do you want to live to be 90, my father said.
You'll be shitting in a diaper, and some poor lady from
Haiti will have to roll you over.

I love my wife. Lately, I've been considering lifting weights
Giving up red meat, cutting down on smokes.

When we almost bounced at the bank
And I was pulling out what little hair I had,
She said: You smell like cinnamon.
Kissed my shoulder, derailed my rage.

I teach her the names of birds, of wild flowers.
She is taking her crow bar of love and prying my fingers loose
From mistrust. It ain't easy. I don't trust the ground underneath me.
I've been there when it collapsed.
I don't trust the Dow Jones or the soft pillow under my head
Or, sometimes, even her love.
Late at night, when the ghosts of my parents
Walk across the kitchen floor,
When I am weeping because the losses are in—not of
This loss in things,

She rolls over from a dream, clamps me to the bed with her legs
Says: Hi.

It is 2 a.m. She goes to bed at ten and sleeps till ten.
I go to bed at two and sleep until five.
We are on different shifts. Having googled ostrich,
And Tony Curtis, and Lisbon, and García Frederico Lorca

I try to lie down beside her again. I hold her
Head like a football in my arms.
She buries her face in my chest.
I say I'm afraid, Emily. I'm not used to anything that stays.
I don't know what to do with staying.
She says: Get me a glass of water.

Girl with Umbrella

Rain splashes the yellow school bus
and the enormous eyelashes
of a girl who has been twirling her umbrella,
balancing it on her nose, who now
watches it torn by the wind—

she thinks of it all day—its ruined body
rolling down the rain-swept street.

How casually things break: the sky, for example, or
the body of Christ. Amen,

her own heart is pounding, racing
as the boy next to her touches her foot with his own
under the library table
casually, not knowing the weight of his touch—

how heavy everything is—and all at once,
and how she must clench her eyelids closed to remember
her body veering, the umbrella handle poised lightly on her nose,
her arms outstretched, staggering under
that whole weight of the sky—
the rain's relentless applause.

Green Light

In the dark, the green light glows from my father's radio.
Outside, rain, and the sound of rain under 18 wheels.
Along the highway, the truckers speak to each other in long
all-night drawls of almost finished sentences. I think the
voice of the midnight universe is always vaguely Southern:
West Virginia, North Carolina, Shiloh, Vicksburg, moving
on up all the way to Cleveland, and down to some great
swamp where dead cedars rise, where a heron barely stirs.
I am thinking how pain calcifies in the heart, how great
cathedrals in the cave of someone's closed eyes are being
formed—drop by drop, on the limestone walls of trout
streams, in the caves of Kentucky, all the way through to
Pennsylvania. Is a man alone, stretched out upon the pallet
of his bed? Is he ever less than a landscape, an outcropping
of rocks, voices, wires, the sharp elbows of waitresses at 3
a.m.? No one reduces me save business as usual and if you
have enough time, my father said, enough time to swallow
your own spit, you might hear the universe speaking to
you—its endless patter, its voice in the stones, a great rock
along 81 south whose silence is song. Do not trust the junk-
ies of that more civil silence. They are loud with their seren-
ity, but the violent bear it away—the trucks moving along
the highway in the rain. When my mother died I crept into
his room, his head down and cradled in his hands. Long
ago, and long ago, and long ago, and long ago. Grief, don't
let me know you cheaply. I put my arms around you—and I
am not afraid.

Love Poem for My Daughter Clare

Can't sleep. Tonight while my wife went out, I stayed home with my daughter and we lay on some pillows on the living room floor and watched TV—mostly old shows. She is making sounds all the time now and I love it. She talks with her hands. I give her a shot of formula and then I swig my water. We lie there and she jabbers away. After she and my wife both fell asleep I wished my life could always be so simple and so clean. I am not the same person anywhere that I am with my daughter.

It is overwhelming, and sometimes it frightens me. Outside there is all that dark, the buds of the trees are so tight and full of promise, and yet everything teeters, is both on the brink of spilling and of being spilled. I saw a purple finch today. I whispered this fact to my daughter as she jabbered away to *Everyone Loves Raymond.* She will never remember that I whispered that to her. I want the love I feel for my daughter to be like the art work done by the artisans in the eves of Chartres. They did their best carvings where no one but God would ever see them. I tell her: "Someday you will not know I love you. Someday, you will take me for granted, and so I embrace being lost to memory and to sight so that even the dark can love you, and the tight buds of the trees, and it doesn't matter—all this love grown outward like a prayer: it will endure until I am erased in you, and you are erased in whatever you choose to love. I am so incredibly, impossibly overwhelmed and grateful that you exist upon this earth.

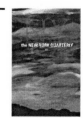

CPSIA information can be obtained at www.ICGtesting.com
Printed in the USA
BVOW02s1921151013

333827BV00002B/6/P